SHINE ON

SHINE ON

Raising Our Kids with Disabilities to Lead *Bright, Happy* Lives

Cynthia Schulz

Copyright © 2025 by Cynthia Schulz

All rights reserved. No part of this book may be reproduced, stored in a retrieval system or transmitted, in any form or by any means, without the prior written consent of the publisher, except in the case of brief quotations, embodied in reviews and articles.

Permission has been obtained to reproduce the lyrics from "The Hiring Chain" performed by Sting and produced by CoorDown, Small New York, Stabbiolo Music, and Indiana Production.

Cataloguing in publication information is available from Library and Archives Canada.
ISBN 978-1-77458-508-5 (paperback)
ISBN 978-1-77458-509-2 (ebook)

Page Two
pagetwo.com

Edited by Emily Schultz
Copyedited by Melissa Kawaguchi
Cover design by Cameron McKague
Interior design by Taysia Louie
and Peter Cocking

CynthiaSchulz.com

For Rick, the perfect dad for our children

———————

Thank you to those parents who shared their stories and their children's stories with me. Thanks also to the many professionals whose work benefiting the developmental disability community is featured in these pages. I aim to present an authentic portrait of families living well with developmental disabilities every day. You helped me draw that portrait.

Contents

Preface *1*

CHAPTER 1
It's Not the End of the World, but It Feels Like It *5*

CHAPTER 2
Let the Learning Begin *21*

CHAPTER 3
Inclusion Lifts Us All Up *37*

CHAPTER 4
Gifted and Talented? You Bet! *53*

CHAPTER 5
This Life Is Difficult *71*

CHAPTER 6
Think in New Ways *91*

CHAPTER 7
Say Hello to Giggles and Goofiness *109*

CHAPTER 8
Thank You to the Trailblazers *123*

CHAPTER 9
Suddenly, They're Adults *139*

CHAPTER 10
Love Triumphs *161*

Acknowledgements *181*
Notes *183*

Preface

BLINK, AND SHE'S AN ADULT. Awesome at 40, our daughter Noelle, nicknamed Noni, is the inspiration for this book and proof you can live a wonderful life with disabilities.

Her story is dotted with bright spots: Attending public school, making friends, learning to swim and ride a bike, going to homecoming and prom, graduating with her class, hanging out with her siblings, working at our local grocery store.

Pretty remarkable for a kid who can't read, write, button clothes, tie shoes, brush teeth, or cross the street safely. That's our Noni Baloney Macaroni, as we affectionately call her, short on cognitive and motor ability and long on personality.

My husband and I are parents of four—Kale, Noni, Jacy, and Trent—all young adults today. Never did we hope for a child with disabilities. No parent does. When it happened to us as young parents, it changed everything. What we didn't know then, however, is that it would change our lives *for the better*.

When Noni at 2 years old was diagnosed with intellectual and motor disabilities after missing many early milestones, our world turned upside down. The revelation was crushing, suffocating, heart stopping.

We were scared for her and for what lay ahead. What would her future look like? And our future too?

Not at all what I wanted for her or for me. I prayed it was a mistake. I prayed it would go away. I fell into what I term "the dark days," when I struggled to put one foot in front of the other.

At times like this, the days drone on, until somewhere deep down you know you can't stay sad forever. Darkness begins to lift. Heartache melts in time. I promise. I wish back then I could have had a glimpse of Noni now, because it would have soothed me to see her grown, beautiful inside and out, healthy and happy and fulfilled, loving and beloved, as she is today.

Now, no more thoughts of what might have been. No more wishing it away. I've found my peace. This life is hard, but I wouldn't trade it for anything. I'm eternally grateful God's plan for our family included her.

Today, I meet many young parents of children with disabilities who are where I was many years ago, starting from scratch on a rough road with no map. In these pages, I share the routes we and others have taken to get where we are now, hoping to enlighten and encourage those called to this journey.

This book is especially for parents as well as for siblings, grandparents, aunts, uncles, cousins, friends, and anyone who loves someone with a developmental disability. It's also for those interested in taking an empathetic peek into the unvarnished lives of families raising atypical kids.

Myriad disorders—well known or unknown, common or rare, severe or mild, inherited or random—cause lifelong disabilities in children. The term "developmental" or "neurodevelopmental" disabilities commonly refers to brain disorders affecting intellect, language, motor skills, or behavior, often in combination.

The individuals you will meet in this book are vastly different, but one commonality almost all share is intellectual disability. While this condition varies in severity, it often means these individuals require a great deal of assistance from others. Their dependence is a job that falls to parents thrust into the role of caregivers, likely for a lifetime.

In the United States, the term "special needs" is a catch-all phrase that covers multiple handicaps and is useful when there's no need to get into specific medical terminology. Phraseology around disabilities is particular to place and time—continually evolving and debated, leaving well-intentioned people afraid to say the wrong thing.

Being sensitive to language is important. It's more precise and delicate, for example, to describe someone as *having* autism, not *being* autistic, since individuals are multidimensional, not solely defined by disability. No term fully captures someone's uniqueness.

Disability is part of being human, according to the World Health Organization (WHO), since almost everyone will temporarily or permanently experience disability at some point in life. WHO estimates those experiencing significant disability at 1.3 billion people, about 16 percent of the global population or one in six of us, making people with disabilities the world's largest minority.

These figures correlate with the U.S. Centers for Disease Control and Prevention statistics, indicating one in six children aged 3 through 17 in the United States have one or more developmental disabilities. It's no surprise to parents, however, that society and education systems are often not built to accommodate these students.

Parents catapulted into this land of special needs quickly learn it's no place for the meek. Time comes to turn off the waterworks and bring on the warrior within, because you'll have to fight for this kid.

Brace yourself to be told no, over and over again, but don't take no for an answer. No way. No how. Hooey. Horsefeathers. Bananas. Crackers. Applesauce. Baloney.

In our house, we say, "Baloney macaroni!" It's a nice way of saying "Hell no!"

Bring new ideas, push for change, rewrite the rules, be a force to reckon with until you hear "Yes." That's how you shape a wonderful life with special needs.

When parents step out of their comfort zones and stand up for their children's rights and best interests, kids with all kinds of disabilities blossom. Their stories fill the pages of this book, and you will learn from them, as I have.

Our daughter today is healthy and joyful, with purpose in her life. She lights up our family in ways no one else can and makes us all better humans. The person she has become is the answer to our prayers.

It's Not the End of the World, but It Feels Like It

*Here is a woman I will bless with a child less than perfect.
She doesn't realize it yet, but she is to be envied.*
ERMA BOMBECK, American humorist and syndicated columnist

ERMA BOMBECK'S prescient words do come true: "She will never take for granted a spoken word. She will never consider a step ordinary. When her child says 'Momma' for the first time, she will be present at a miracle and know it!"

Miracles are what we live for, and they happen.

It wasn't long before I began to witness tiny steps, one little miracle after another. When I saw my daughter throw a ball for the first time at 5 years old, a motor-release skill babies typically master before the age of 1, I was present at a miracle and rejoiced in it!

Your child will bring you miracles and joys you never imagined.

In the following excerpts from the column first published in 1993, Bombeck visualized God hovering over Earth selecting instruments for propagation with great care before passing a name to an angel:

"Give her a handicapped child."

The angel is curious. "Why this one, God? She's so happy."

"Exactly," smiles God. "Could I give a handicapped child to a mother who does not know laughter?"

"But has she patience?" asks the angel.

"I don't want her to have too much patience or she will drown in a sea of self-pity and despair. Once the shock and resentment wear off, she'll handle it.

"I will permit her to see clearly the things I see... ignorance, cruelty, prejudice... and rise above them. She will never be alone. I will be at her side every minute of every day of her life because she is doing my work..."

Maybe you just received a diagnosis for your child. Maybe you're struggling to accept the reality. Maybe no one told you all of the things your child *will* do.

Hold tight to the promise your child will bring you miracles and joys you never imagined.

Tell me gently and stay with me awhile

My toddler's clinical diagnosis—mental retardation—arrived by mail. Those two words jumped off the page and hit me between the eyes as I sank to my knees.

Forty years later, we know this diagnosis by more palatable terminology: Intellectual disability, developmental disability, or special needs. No matter how you phrase it, this news for parents is knee buckling, and delivering it is no job for the post office.

The nomenclature and the delivery, however, were a sad sign of the times. I had been cooking dinner, occasionally stirring a pot of spaghetti sauce, while Kale and Noni, 4 and 2, played nearby. I opened that letter from the neurologist, never expecting it would contain Noni's test results, when I took the blow.

In that moment, I needed arms around me, a human heart to share my grief, someone to reassure me it would be all right. But postage stamps don't bring care and compassion.

I was a mess. A shattered-in-a-million-pieces mess. A tears-mixed-with-snot-running-down-my-face mess. An I-can't-figure-out-how-to-get-dinner-on-the-table mess.

I sobbed myself to sleep. For days. For weeks. For my baby girl. For me.

In good time, with a calmer heart, I stopped grieving the loss of the child she would never be. I began to see clearly the child she was *meant to be* and the mother I was meant to be. Never did I imagine her potential to be our family's indisputable greatest blessing.

I wish some professional had shared this intrinsic bonus missing from the cold diagnosis.

What causes developmental disabilities is sometimes a mystery, as it was with Noni. She was late to reach major milestones. She took her first step at 20 months—we had a party—and she toddled unsteadily at 24 months. She uttered few words. It was time for testing.

The young mom in me was hopeful. Maybe numerous ear infections as a baby temporarily affected her hearing and balance, slowing her development. Maybe we'd find something we could "fix" and she'd catch up.

Until receiving the news, I hadn't let my mind go where this diagnosis took me, and the reality hit me hard. The root cause of her delayed development, however, was undetermined.

Early intervention was hard to find when she was little. Public schools didn't yet offer preschool for youngsters with special needs. That came years later, too late for Noni. We found a private preschool for her, a very expensive option and our only one.

Needed therapies—speech, physical, and occupational—for nebulous developmental disabilities with unknown causes were not covered then by health insurance.

Noni's timing couldn't have been better, though, when it came to inclusion of kids with special needs in public schools in the 1980s. She got lucky as a kindergartner to participate in our state's first pilot program for inclusion, where she learned alongside typical peers.

The power of inclusion can't be overstated. Involving kids with disabilities in typical childhood experiences has proved to pave the way for them to live full lives.

At age 30, Noni underwent genetic testing, which finally pinpointed the cause of her disability: A brain-development defect known as CASK gene disorder, discovered in 2008. Little is known about this rare condition, but several researchers around the world are working to understand more.

Having this knowledge has since connected us with fewer than three hundred families across the world raising children also affected by this condition. We're no longer alone in this struggle. A Facebook group keeps us in the know and provides a safe space to ask questions, seek suggestions, and occasionally vent.

Because Noni is one of the oldest identified with this rare disorder, I can offer parents of youngsters and teens a glimpse into her bright adult life with CASK and encourage them to keep their hopes high.

Finding out the cause has been a long time coming. Now, there's no more wondering. No more flying blind. No more fearing I may have been to blame, a worry mothers of kids with special needs are good at.

Knowing about CASK, however, doesn't solve its destructive effects on our daughter or change our daily lives as parents continuing to raise an adult child with disabilities. Today, we are abundantly thankful for Noni—daughter, sister, granddaughter, aunt, niece, cousin, and friend. We wouldn't change a thing.

Except for that letter.

You're not alone

Grief is completely normal and without escape when you learn your child has a disability. Parents must go through it to make it to the other side.

Nothing anyone can say or do will make the problem go away. No silver lining to be found in this new reality.

Mom and Dad need consoling. At this moment, they're thinking about all the things their child *won't* do—not all they will do. I'll always remember the perceptive words of a neighbor when it happened to us: "The only difference between Noni and the rest of our kids is now you know what you're dealing with. Our children will all have issues as they grow up; we just don't know yet what they'll be. One thing I know for sure," he said, "*you* can do this."

Those words soothed and buoyed me.

A disability diagnosis conveyed with compassion and hope is what parents need, according to these moms of children with a CASK diagnosis:

- Sarah still clings to the caring words of daughter Tara's neurologist: "You need to grieve the loss of the child you dreamed of and accept the child you have been blessed with."

- An enlightened geneticist advised Gina, "Keep the bar high for Angela. She's going to write her own story." The geneticist didn't begin with a list of all the things she likely would never be able to do. Years later, Gina reflects, "I hold that uplifting thought close to my heart every day."

- "It's not just what someone says, but how they say it," offers Graham's mom, Allie. "Our neurogeneticist showed us so much humanity and compassion while delivering the news. It helped soften the blow."

Eliza Factor, author of *Strange Beauty*, a memoir of her family's experiences raising a child with multiple disabilities, was comforted by a friend's perspective that most young parents starting families were in a "honeymoon period," while she and her husband were "getting the full brunt of parenthood all at once."

Factor, who's firstborn, Felix, has periventricular leukomalacia, autism, and cerebral palsy, treasured that comment because it "interwove our experience with everyone else's. We weren't that different; we were just getting it all at once."

She soon learned she also needed the company of parents of kids with disabilities who "get it" without saying a word. It led her to turn an empty classroom in a co-op preschool in Brooklyn, New York, into a nonprofit play center for kids with disabilities as well as their siblings and parents.

As her nonprofit, Extreme Kids & Crew, has grown, Factor has grown with it in ways she never could have imagined as that once despairing young mother. "It has unleashed something in me: a quiet joy, that deep down feeling of not being alone."

"It's in moments of vulnerability that we either become insular or accept that we need others," said *Grey's Anatomy* actress Caterina Scorsone when her daughter Pippa was born with Down syndrome. "Parents of other kids with special needs became like instant family." Instant family aptly describes how your circle will expand with a whole new set of kindred spirits to lean on. They will become your village once you let them in.

Closer to home, family and friends who want to reach out to you may be hesitant, unsure how to comfort or support you, afraid to say the wrong thing. Open your heart to them. Allow yourself to take comfort in the empathy of those close to you who feel your pain.

A warm smile, a tight hug, a brimming tear, flowers, a note, an invite to dinner, an offer to babysit, a cup of coffee, a long walk, or the promise of undying support demonstrate *I'm here for you.*

When Mom and Dad need it most.

Say goodbye to your dreams

As you look upon your sleeping baby in her crib when you're waiting for critical medical test results, it's time to make a pact with your supreme being.

Mine went something like this: "Please, God, let me keep her. Let her be healthy and happy. Let her life have meaning. That's it. That's enough."

Letting go of all the what-could-have-beens for your child is wrenching, but the thought of losing her is far worse. You know this when you're on your knees begging for only what matters most. Will she be a doctor, lawyer, teacher, scientist, engineer, artist, author, actress? No. Lofty dreams are not to be for this one, and we can live without them.

Hmm... if only what matters most is enough for this child, is it enough for my other kids too?

Our hopes for her will be simpler, like walking and talking. When, with hard work, she reaches a milestone, like walking and talking, we find ourselves wildly celebrating because health, happiness, and meaning would have been enough.

When she doesn't learn to read, a huge disappointment, I remind myself I didn't ask for reading. We discover it's not the end of the world.

Hmm... if what matters most is enough for this child, is it enough for my other kids too?

For me, the answer turned out to be yes.

This eye-opener cooled my jets about little things, like my son's B in Spanish on his otherwise straight-A report card. He said to me, "Mom, it's Spanish. My goal is to forget everything I ever learned in Spanish as soon as I never have to take another Spanish class. I could actually apply myself and get an A or do nothing and get a B. Mom, it's Spanish."

Point taken, though hard for me to take. But I can let go of perfection because my child with special needs has made me more attuned to what's essential. Today, my prayer for all my children is for health, happiness, and meaning.

Anything more is a bonus.

Should we have another child?

It's a big question.

Getting a disability diagnosis or a sense your child is struggling often comes when young couples are still planning how big their families will be.

My husband and I always wanted a bunch of kids.

When we learned our second born had developmental disabilities, the unexpected diagnosis gave us pause. We were consumed with meeting this child's every need. Could we handle another?

We had lots of questions and few answers at the time. Could whatever caused Noni's disability be hereditary? Was it a fluke? We had no way of knowing. What we were sure of, though, was that her typically developing older brother, Kale, was a godsend to his sister.

Ultimately, we took a leap of faith and, indeed, saying yes to having another (and another) was among our best decisions ever, and the greatest gift we could give to Noni.

Bringing home a new baby girl followed by a new baby boy forced me to focus on something other than Noni's disabilities. It restored balance to our family. Disabilities became just one part of our busy lives. It taught me to ask for help when my hands were full.

Siblings work around her disabilities, finding ways to fill her life with fun.

Crazy as it seems, expanding our family was the right move for us.

How do her three siblings feel about growing up with a sister with special needs? First words out of their mouths:

- Big brother: "It's my normal."
- Little sister: "I don't know anything different."
- Baby brother: "No big deal."

I pry. Tell me more about the pros and cons:

- "No cons."
- "All good."
- "Seriously, Mom, it's no big deal."

As youngsters, this trio expressed amusing advantages to having a sister with special needs:

- "When we all pitch in to buy something big, we can tap into her money too. Mom, we're including her!"
- "We can go right to the front of the line at Cedar Point when she's with us. Don't worry, Mom. She's gonna love the roller coasters!"

- "We get extra turns playing video games. We unplug her controller, and she doesn't know the difference. Mom, she's happy just hanging out with us."

She is, and they are too. I can look back and know for certain the years of education, therapies, inclusion, accommodations, and advocacy, all mixed with love, got her and us to this place. Her siblings work around her disabilities, finding ways to fill her life with fun. In return, their empathy muscles get a good workout, making them more caring beings.

In the process, I see each sibling relating differently to this sister:

- Big brother: A big tease but a bigger guardian angel.

- Little sister: Special needs get no special treatment from this one. Sisters!

- Baby brother: Happy-go-lucky and happy to let her tag along with his friends. No big deal.

Ah, but it is.

Work your magic, baby

Individuals with special needs possess superpowers, the kind that make the world better. Early on, parents often don't see it. They're consumed with trying to understand a dreadful diagnosis, taking care of a child disabled by it, and working through grief that comes in waves.

Soon enough, though, come melting moments to make everything all right. Parents whose children, like my daughter, have CASK gene disorder and have come to know each other via a supportive Facebook group, the CASK Gene Parent Support Group, shared how their kids have a way of bringing out the best in others:

- After he's tucked into his own big-boy bed at night, brother Bo tiptoes into baby Ellie's room and climbs into her crib, where Mom finds the two siblings in the morning in a cozy snuggle. "She wants me in there," insists Bo, who keeps a watchful eye over his little sister with special needs. As they cuddle in the crib, he reads stories, shares stuffed animals, and plays games with Ellie. "In the morning, I sing her a song," he tells Mom. "It's called, 'I love my sister and she loves me.' She likes that song."

- Since his wife died a few years ago, a bereaved great-grandfather has kept her seat at the table empty whenever guests come by. Until little Taryn visited. She cozied up to Grippy, and instantly the two were giggling and being silly together. When he invited her to sit next to him, Taryn hopped into Granny's seat and made Grippy happier than he'd been in a long time.

- At a child's birthday party, a curious youngster asked Abbie's mom what was on her daughter's face. Mom gently explained that Abbie sometimes needs a little extra help breathing. The stickers on her face hold tubing that gives her oxygen. The little inquisitor understood. When someone asked what she hopes to be when she grows up, she answered, "I'm going to be a doctor," then pointing to Abbie, "for her."

- When fifth-grader Eliana needed assistance in the school hallway, three girls jumped to her aid. The three had a falling out months before but managed to set aside their differences for Eliana. In that moment, Eliana was the catalyst the girls needed to let go of their hard feelings and mend their friendship.

- Grandma with dementia refused to eat or walk. Her teenage great-granddaughter, Shania, patiently retaught her the basics of how to eat and walk with her walking frame. Many others had tried but failed to break through Grandma's dementia. Only Shania, with her special needs, could reach her.

To be touched by them is a blessing.

As my father always told me about my own daughter with CASK, "She brings us all closer to God."

"OPTIMISMS" TO LIVE BY

IT'S NOT the end of the world when you find out your child has special needs, but sometimes it feels like it. Take time to process, to grieve, to fall apart. In time, you'll pick yourself up, put one foot in front of the other, and move forward. Your burning love will fuel you with the energy and strength you'll need to make a good life for your child.

Let the Learning Begin

*The most important thing people did for
me was to expose me to new things.*
TEMPLE GRANDIN, distinguished animal behaviorist,
professor, author, speaker

FOR MANY of us, Temple Grandin is one of the first names to come to mind when we hear the word "autism." Growing up in the 1950s, Grandin didn't have the resources available to many children today, but she has spoken and written extensively about the strong support she benefited from.

I had people in my life who didn't give up on me: My mother, my aunt, my science teacher. I had a nanny who spent all day playing turn-taking games with me. During meals, I was taught table manners. When a social or manners mistake was made, Mother never screamed "No" or "Stop it." Instead, she calmly gave me the instruction of what I should do:

- *If I twirled my fork around above my head, she said, "Put your fork on your plate."*

- *If I ate mashed potatoes with my fingers, she said, "Use the fork."*
- *If I forgot to say thank you, she would give me a cue and say, "You forgot to say (pause)."*

I love Grandin's advice for parents today, because it's practical and builds self-confidence:

- Don't get so worried about deficits. Build up strengths, life skills, and work skills, which can turn into a job.
- Be flexible in school with kids with differently abled brains or uneven skills.
- Have high but reasonable expectations and stretch kids slightly outside their comfort zones.
- Teach kids how to shop, shake hands, take coats, order food at a restaurant, walk the dog, volunteer, or, as in Grandin's case, clean horse stalls.

"Being recognized for doing a job well done as a child," Grandin reflected, "improved my self-esteem."

Learning a little means a lot

"I'm not sure what your child is getting out of this." Sound familiar? Every parent of every kid with developmental disabilities hears these words and cringes.

The universal answer is *a little bit.*

I didn't take it well when Noni's safety-town teacher approached me saying, "I suppose you can keep bringing her if you want. Frankly, I don't think she's getting anything out of it."

"That's probably why God gave her to me, not you," I snapped. "See you tomorrow."

It's safety town, for heaven's sake! A two-week summer program before kids start kindergarten to teach them basic safety. They pedal little cars and coupes around a town of miniature buildings and houses, obeying stop signs, traffic lights, crosswalks, police officers, and firefighters. If you're 5 years old, it's a blast.

Apparently, this teacher was exasperated because what my daughter learns today often vanishes from her memory by tomorrow. Welcome to my world! I blame it on midnight elves erasing the blackboard in her brain as she sleeps, so she can start fresh each morning with a blank slate.

By comparison, Noni's siblings absorb a world of knowledge practically on autopilot. Do we treat our typical children differently than our child with disabilities? You bet, because their individual needs are poles apart. Our parenting philosophy is not to treat our kids the same but to give each child what he or she needs. For families like ours, same is not equal.

Too bad, so sad for little sister Jacy, routinely responsible for straightening both sides of the bedroom she shares with Noni. Why? Because she can and her big sister cannot.

"Not fair," she complained once, launching me into a hellfire sermon.

"What's fair at the moment of birth for one sister to receive a litany of talents and gifts and the other to draw a short straw? From this perspective, young lady, tidying up is a privilege! You're welcome."

Did someone slam the bedroom door? (She better be cleaning up in there.)

"Same is not equal" applies to school too. For example, we let go of math facts and science experiments for Noni because that knowledge will never stick enough to matter for her future. Unfortunately for her siblings, we're all about math and science.

Higher learning may be the goal for most kids in school, but not for all, and particularly not for those with limited intellectual capacity. Just by being there, however, they learn a tiny bit and have a chance to experience field trips, musical performances, dances, and sports events. They build social skills and feel a sense of belonging.

Belonging? That notion went right over the head of the safety-town teacher who surmised our daughter's participation in this pre-kindergarten summer ritual was a waste of time.

"She's moving the little cars pretty nicely with her feet," I pointed out, appreciating her motor progress. "She's making friends too. How about that!" So what if she's not stopping at stop signs and is eagerly taking candy from strangers?

Learning for this child is painfully slow, requiring lots of repetition for her to understand and remember an itty bit. Stop signs and stranger danger will take more years of repetition to stick.

For now, we're proud to report she finished the course and graduated from safety town with all the other kids, excitedly waving her certificate in the air.

And waving, you guessed it, another shameless handful of candy.

Don't let the bus leave without me

In a conversation with my toddler's neurologist, I asked what I might expect for Noni in the future. "Well, I don't think she'll be riding a yellow school bus with the other kids, if that's what you're asking me," he said.

I didn't see that coming! She was just a baby, and I wasn't thinking that far ahead. No school bus for Noni? Now I had another dashed hope to cry over.

Nobody, nobody, nobody knows for sure. And times change.

I held on to my hope for her to ride the school bus. Then the inclusion movement happened, and she did.

Inclusion, fortified by a hefty push from warrior parents Elaine and Scott, paved the way for their daughter, Alana, to ride the bus too. Alana has HUWE1 gene disorder, a condition so rare fewer than fifty children with this diagnosis have been reported in the medical literature.

On the first day of school, neighborhood friends and their camera-toting parents gathered at the bus stop, where all the buzz was about new kindergartner Alana. Who would get to sit next to her on her first ride? "Pick me! Pick me!" the kids clamored.

Moms suggested they start with the oldest and rotate each day according to age. Good solution. Alana's bus aide would be permanently relegated to the seat behind her. Perfect spot.

All aboard. No one left behind.

Henry's mother, Emily, watches him board the school bus each day, waving as her seventh grader with autism finds his seat and waves back through the window. Even though her child is able and old enough to board the bus by himself, Emily wouldn't miss this ritual. It took years for Henry to learn to wave. At first he waved backward with his palm in his face. Today, his happy wave is a miracle that doesn't escape his mom.

Like Alana and Henry, Noni rode the school bus with her siblings and neighborhood friends. We've got years of first-day-of-school pictures at the bus stop to prove it.

And a new neurologist.

Beware the flames of burning love

I cringe every time someone suggests my daughter can't or won't do something.

I listen politely and try to be respectful. For example, our parish priest explained to me why my first grader could *not* attend a weekly hour-long religion class:

- Because other parishes—not ours—have classes for children like your daughter.
- Because our teachers don't have special training.
- Because we've never done it before.

My comeback:

- Our family belongs to *this* parish.
- If teachers aren't sure what to do with Noni, they can ask another student. These kids go to public school together all day long and know how to include her in a lesson.
- Let's see, you're teaching Christianity here. Why not consider her a living laboratory in the classroom for the kids to practice what you preach?
- By the way, I didn't major in special education, and God gave her to me anyway. He, apparently, had faith in me.

But not this priest. He made it clear: His house. His rules.

Finding the nerve to break his rules came to me by way of a story I heard at an inclusion conference about another young mother desperate for her child with multiple profound disabilities to attend the neighborhood elementary school.

The school said no, no, and no. But this mom wouldn't hear it. On the first day of kindergarten, she rolled her little guy into the classroom, parked his wheelchair, and headed home.

Later that morning, a rattled school official called Mom. A hasty morning fire drill on that very first day of school proved her son's presence in the classroom was a fire hazard. Unable to get him out of the building in time to meet code, they concluded he could not safely attend school.

Truth is, they had shortsightedly never incorporated a wheelchair into their drills and were caught unprepared.

Mom dug in, did her research, and discovered there had never been a fire in the eighty-five-year-old school building. She concluded the odds were with her.

Next day, she rolled her son back into school, parked him in his classroom, and this time headed to the principal's office carrying a signed release reading: *In the event of a fire, let him burn.*

Those scorching words set me on fire!

Following this mom's example, I dropped off my daughter with her older brother on the first day of religion class, in spite of the priest's reservations. I instructed Kale to walk Noni to her classroom, introduce her to the teacher, pick her up after class, and meet me at the very same spot in the parking lot.

Once my kids entered the school, I drove away and didn't look back, because I was not taking no for an answer. I repeated this routine every week.

I never heard a peep, not until the priest approached me at the end of the school year. "I owe you an apology," he confessed. "I didn't think it could work but, by God, it did. Shame on me."

There's no shame in opening your mind and arms to a child of God.

Great teachers are a godsend

"Wouldn't you like to see your daughter in a regular education class learning with typical kids?" posed Noni's kindergarten teacher, Mrs. Radey.

If only it were possible, I thought. The radical notion was beyond my wildest dreams. The year was 1989, the infancy of the inclusion movement. Mrs. Radey, a passionate champion for kids with disabilities, had bigger, bolder visions than I did. Was she a genius? Or zanier than me?

The concept of teaching children with and without special needs together was radical in the 1980s. Open-minded proponents collided with kicking-and-screaming critics, and bureaucrats constructed high hurdles. But Mrs. Radey and other teachers like her wouldn't take no for an answer.

The movement shone a bright light on a population of children left behind. More than thirty-five years later, inclusion is turning out capable young adults with disabilities, like my daughter and so many others.

Early on, as a young mother, I was reticent to make waves, grateful for whatever education the schools would provide my child with multiple disabilities. My timid approach soon vanished with the realization that Noni had every right to an education. But to ensure her needs were met, I had to advocate for her and become an activist.

We hitched our wagon to Mrs. Radey's star and let her show us the way. So fortunate were we that she came along at the very beginning of our education journey. Her influence steered us from start to finish.

In the words of Temple Grandin, who speaks from firsthand experience, "I cannot emphasize enough the importance of a good teacher. If you find a good teacher, hang on to him or her tight."

Third grade brought another giant step in our inclusion odyssey. Our daughter jumped ship from her faraway public school, which served a contingent of kids with special needs, to our nearby neighborhood school with her siblings, where she would be its first and only student with multiple developmental disabilities.

Hello, Mr. Zuccaro, a young teacher up for a challenge, who flung open his classroom door for her and many others to follow.

Probably riddled with second thoughts, he asked us nervously, "Are you going to be mad if she doesn't learn to read in my class?"

"Do you disappear into a phone booth and emerge with superpowers?" I quipped. "Because that's what it will take."

When he expressed fear of making a mistake, we assured him, "Never fear. You will, but no matter how hard you try, you'll never make as many mistakes as we do."

As curriculum in middle school and high school transitioned to focus on single subjects, we kept our focus on teachers. For Noni's inclusion classes, we chose teachers who wanted her in their classrooms, no matter what the subject. We knew her teachers would make all the difference.

What Mr. Zuccaro, Mrs. Radey, and many more maverick teachers and aides instill in their welcoming classrooms goes beyond reading, writing, and arithmetic. Or science, technology, engineering, and math.

Kindness and acceptance are also put to the test here. In inclusive classrooms, measurable outcomes for my daughter take the form of coveted invitations—to play together during recess, to attend birthday parties and

Great teachers know good hearts in the classroom are as important as good grades.

---

playdates, to be a partner on a field trip, to sit together at the assembly, to belong.

Great teachers know good hearts in the classroom are as important as good grades.

Confessions of a buzzkill mom

With my firstborn, I admit I thought I must be a pretty good mom for raising such a smart and talented little boy. Then along came Noni, who injected me with a dose of humility.

These two children of the same parents cover the spectrum—one labeled talented and gifted, the other multi-handicapped—for whatever labels in education are worth.

When the time came to meet Kale's teachers at elementary-school parent-teacher conferences, I was eager to hear how well my bright and easygoing son was doing. I got an unexpected earful.

Imagine my startle when the school specialist for the gifted informed me of a new movement afoot in public education threatening the well-being of my son and all gifted students. "It's called inclusion," she explained and presented a protest petition for me to sign.

Did I hear her right? Obviously, this woman doesn't know her audience!

Hmm, I thought to myself, perhaps with a smidge of mean-spiritedness, let's have a little fun with this. "Tell me more," I urged.

She dug a deeper hole as I listened, straight-faced but seething underneath. Her position: Kids with disabilities in the classroom will deprive gifted students of the special attention they need.

Never, not once, have I considered my son needy of special attention. He learns on cruise control, absorbing knowledge with ease. I have a clear picture of special needs, and it doesn't resemble him.

"You know me as Kale's mom," I piped up. "Let me introduce myself to you as Noni's mom. She is the inclusion student you speak of."

How's that for sucking the air out of the room?

I wasn't concerned in the least about my son sharing a classroom with kids with disabilities. Quite the contrary.

As inclusion specialist and author of *Inclusion in Action* Nicole Eredics points out, "The biggest risk of *not* including a child with developmental disabilities is that we limit *everyone's* potential as human beings." She offers teachers this unconventional perspective:

Not every child in your class reads at the exact same level. Nor do they do math, write, or even act at the same developmental level. Not every child in your class can write a complex sentence or identify all the states on a map. The fact is, your "typical" class isn't so typical.

Inclusion, it turns out, gave Kale a valuable opportunity to use his talents and gifts not just to get ahead himself but to serve others. He had a knack for helping classmates better understand math, a subject hard for some but easy for him.

Thanks to classmates with special needs, kids with talents and gifts have an opportunity to model acceptance and blossom as leaders, preparing them well for bright futures. Thanks to typical classmates, kids with special needs have role models and friends to learn from.

So, no, thank you. No petition signing for this mom.

Because every student in an inclusive classroom learns life lessons in humanity.

When bullies become buddies

We hear plenty about bullying in schools and online, and it's important to have these conversations, but our experience has been quite the opposite. Kids can be kind, especially when those with and without disabilities grow up together.

Sometimes friends would ask, "Don't you worry about sending Noni to public school? After all, kids can be cruel."

Fact is, inclusion has the power to turn a bully into a buddy.

In elementary school, Mr. Fudale came up with a brilliant idea, though some might have thought it foolhardy. He invited Noni into his classroom so students could read to her. It was a bold experiment, since the class consisted of six boys, all with behavioral problems. My daughter, likely the most vulnerable student in the school, would be paired with the rowdiest.

Unencumbered by stereotypes or, as some might say, not knowing any better, Noni presumed the best in these boys, not the worst. She was all smiles and sweet as could be to each one.

They didn't disappoint. The boys, infamous for violent outbursts, melted. Gentleness took over as they sat together reading her storybooks and chatting her up.

She loved every minute.

So did they, not just because she doled out generous helpings of respect but also because she needed and appreciated their help. She met their fundamental human need to be needed and kindled the good in them.

Fast forward to middle school years, upon exiting our local big-box store, I hear a young voice say, "Hey, Noni." I turn to see a band of boys with no resemblance to Beaver Cleaver hanging out on skateboards.

My impulse is to pull my daughter close.

"Hey, Matt!" she greets him excitedly and wriggles free from my grasp to approach him and wave.

Walking to our car, I ask her, "Who's that?"

"That's my friend Matt."

"How do you know him?"

"From school."

"Is he a nice boy? Is he nice to you?"

"Oh, yeah!" she says, with a fist pump.

It hits me. It's one of the kids from the reading group. I smile and wave at the boys, realizing I need to get better at not judging a book by its cover.

Luckily, I've got the perfect person to teach me.

"OPTIMISMS" TO LIVE BY

YOUR CHILD will learn. Perhaps just a little bit at a time, but each bit adds up. Kids learn when they go to school, play in the sand, have fun at the park, take swim lessons, use manners, sing, dance to music, suck on a Popsicle, throw a ball, save money, buy a birthday present for Mom, pet a dog, create art, and make a new friend. Exposure is the best teacher.

Inclusion Lifts Us All Up

The woods would be very silent if no birds sang there except those that sang best.
HENRY VAN DYKE, American author, educator, diplomat, and Presbyterian clergyman

FOR ALL the years Noni was in school, this quote lived on our refrigerator, singing the praises of inclusion. Parents of children with developmental disabilities are joining in the chorus.

"If Ellie had the words," says Stephanie Trask, a second-grade teacher whose preschool-aged daughter has CASK gene disorder, "here's how she'd express what inclusion means to her":

- So many teachers, friends, and family who love you
- A chance for you to do the things the other kids are doing because somebody helps you
- A teacher including water activities for stations because you love water or making sure you're included

in the class photo, even when it's hard for you to sit still

- A friend who picks you up to help you get where you want to go
- A brother who talks to you in sentences as if you could talk back
- A bestie who snuggles with you
- A friend who walks with you to Sunday school and, when you get to the stairs, crawls beside you to make sure you don't get left behind. He tells his mom the best thing about Sunday school is Ellie, because "she is so sweet."

It's scary for parents to send their child with disabilities off to school and scarier still to take a leap of faith on inclusion. Little Ellie's impression of preschool mirrors my daughter's positive experiences throughout her school years and beyond.

For Ellie, Noni, and so many others, inclusion works wonders.

How to fit in when you stand out

How can kids with special needs learn in the same classroom with typical students? The answer, in a word, is accommodations.

Adding resources to the inclusion classroom, beginning with indispensable teachers' aides, makes it possible even for students with severe and profound cognitive impairment to learn alongside peers.

It's the happy story of Noni's life.

Fortunately, Noni missed out on mainstreaming, the precursor and flipside of inclusion. The two terms are not synonymous, which comes as a surprise to many people. The difference? One is accommodating, the other is not. For example:

- Mainstreaming of the past cracked opened the door for a fourth grader reading at a first-grade level to go to the first-grade classroom for reading. Who wants to do that?

- Inclusion opens the door wide for a fourth grader to learn to read in his fourth-grade classroom at his own pace, with accommodations and among peers.

For every child with disabilities, whatever academic accommodations are needed in school are spelled out in an individual education plan (IEP) tailored by teachers in collaboration with parents. These all-important planning sessions give parents the power to push for more if their child needs more. And yes, you may need to learn to push.

Besides academics, for example, these students may qualify for school services such as speech therapy, occupational therapy, and physical therapy to help further their development. The confusing world of acronyms starts early in disability circles.

In middle school, Noni took English class. Of all subjects, why English for a nonreader? Because the English

How can kids with special needs learn in the same classroom with typical students? The answer is accommodations.

---

teacher wanted her and was willing to make accommodations for her to be successful. What did those accommodations look like? One aide, two beanbag chairs, picture books, and music.

When the class was reading a Little House on the Prairie chapter book, Noni's aide chose a Little House children's library book for her. Each day, one student was selected to sit with Noni in the beanbag chairs at the back of the room—a treat—and quietly read the book to her, asking questions and pointing out pictures.

Students took seriously the responsibilities of reading to her, teaching her, and being her friend. She loved reading the story over and over and talking about it with her agemates. Sharing a story together is a bonding experience, and comprehension and enjoyment can be more important than being able to identify the words.

When it was time to read biographies and give oral book reports in front of the class, Noni's aide suggested she perform a variation on the theme with a musical report on the life of Gloria Estefan. Genius! This idea played to her strengths since she can remember the lyrics to practically every song, a remarkable splinter skill her classmates are well aware of, listening to her sing every morning and afternoon to the music on the school bus.

On the day of her performance, donned in a miniskirt and with curls in her hair, she shared three quick fun facts about Gloria Estefan, then sang and danced to her hit song "Get on Your Feet." A biography report with a beat, followed by an ovation!

Classmates are also called on to use their creativity to accommodate and include a fellow student with special needs.

Noni's science class divided into small groups to perform an experiment and present it to the class. Her group brainstormed a role for Noni on the project. They met after school at a classmate's house, where she colored mostly outside the lines on a poster showing fire erupting from a volcano. They rehearsed her one-liner in the presentation, a scientific fact now embedded in her brain: Fire comes out of a volcano.

On a family vacation to Hawaii years later, she saw a real volcano and it clicked: Fire comes out of a volcano.

Lesson learned.

Disabilities? Cool!

When baby boomers like me were in school, we had scant vocabulary to explain why some kids were different.

Nobody talked about it in that era, and it wasn't polite to ask.

"Crippled" was the word used to describe someone with cerebral palsy. "Slow" was the expression for intellectual disability. Everything else was hush-hush.

Fast forward through the decades as Chris, a sixth grader in a new middle school, stood up to introduce himself to his new classmates. After telling the class a bit about himself, he added, "Oh, by the way, I have Tourette syndrome. It makes me twitch and shout out sometimes. My eye blinks a lot too, so if you ever think I'm winking at you, I'm not. I can't help it. It just happens. No big deal."

What did the sixth graders think? No big deal. Cool.

No one was left wondering. Chris's words unmasked the mystery and led his classmates to quick understanding and acceptance.

Singer-songwriter Billie Eilish is open about her diagnosis of Tourette syndrome as a child. After experiencing its symptoms for so long, Eilish said it's become a part of her. "I have made friends with it, so now I'm pretty confident in it," she said. By publicly expressing that kind of confidence, she is a model for others managing the involuntary movements and rising above the stigma of this neurological disorder.

Attention deficit disorder is Megan's challenge. Working her first summer job as a teenager behind the counter at McDonald's, she could sense a customer getting impatient with her. "Sir, I have attention deficit disorder. I am doing the best I can. I hope you will be just a little patient with me."

> In today's era of inclusion,
> the conversation has switched from
> "what's wrong" to "what's different."

How's that for disarming!

In today's era of inclusion, the conversation has switched from "what's wrong" to "what's different." Kids are now armed with language to advocate for themselves.

Not all are able to understand or articulate their disability, but those who are benefit from this knowledge. Giving them, and everybody from siblings to friends to relatives, appropriate words to explain their shade of difference is a gift that keeps on giving, as it builds understanding that gets passed on to others.

Famed physicist Stephen Hawking expressed his hope that "this century will mark a turning point for inclusion of people with disabilities in the lives of their societies."

I believe it's happening.

When someone asks me about my daughter, I've got lingo to explain her intellectual and motor disabilities, something she is unable to voice herself. But I like to brag about her capabilities too.

She loves to work, bowl, cycle, swim, listen to music, go to dances, set the table, sort silverware, make her bed, watch *Wheel of Fortune* and guess the color of Vanna's dress, ride in Daddy's truck, bring in the mail, take out the garbage, and put on her pajamas all by herself.

Cool.

Happy to accommodate you

When you make accommodations for one group, you often make it easier for others too.

When you design something specifically for the physically challenged, for example, you wind up designing for everybody. Take curb cuts. They're intended to help wheelchair users maneuver across streets and sidewalks. Far more often, though, we see strollers, bicycles, grocery carts, and even Grandma going this smooth route. Life made easier for many.

When a local elementary school was installing an elevator, we overheard some grumbling: "Can you believe they're spending thousands of dollars for an elevator for one kid?"

Turns out that one kid has plenty of company in the elevator.

Grandparents with achy knees ride that elevator to their grandchildren's classrooms on the upper floors. Students, teachers, and parents who've rolled an ankle, broken a leg, or had foot surgery are grateful for the lift. Carts full of supplies go along for the ride too.

Oversized handicap-accessible bathroom stalls conveniently double as family restrooms for parents whose little ones have to go potty, now. Travelers find them fitting for a quick change of clothes.

Family and gender-neutral bathrooms are a welcome relief for moms of sons and dads of daughters who otherwise might suffer judgmental looks bringing a child of the opposite sex into a bathroom. Kids and adults with special needs may look old enough to use the bathroom by themselves but, in fact, they often need assistance.

How about when your arms are full of groceries or packages? You strike it lucky when you come across that push button on a handicap-accessible door.

My friend sings the praises of Uber for her elderly mother who no longer drives. Surely, seniors are not the target market its creators had in mind, but it's a happy accident.

Kids think handicap-accessible water fountains were made just for them, but dogs know otherwise.

Yummy gummy vitamins designed for children are a solution for adults, like my daughter, who have trouble swallowing pills.

Disposable diapers aren't just for babies.

We all benefit from accommodations, because everybody has special needs sometimes.

Hey, good looking!

I like to think my daughter with disabilities always showed up to school looking snazzy in her matching outfits and stylish hairdos. But on days I was out of town,

Daddy was on his own, with his limited skills at taming hair and matching anything on display.

I call it her "waif of America" look.

Kids with disabilities are cool, and it helps to dress the part. No mismatches, please, for this crowd. I probably went overboard sending Noni off to elementary school, never a day without bows, clips, or ribbons to accessorize her ponytails or french braids. And don't forget the stick-on earrings, a fad of the 1980s.

Kids with and without disabilities can find common ground and exchange compliments when they all look nice. Fashionable clothes and shoes for kids who don't button, zip, or tie are becoming easier to find.

More and more clothing manufacturers are addressing the growing demand for comfortable, on-trend adaptive clothing. Zippered pants for kids in braces or casts; easy-opening magnetic or Velcro closures hiding under buttons; discreet openings for access to G-tubes; and hands-free, slip-in footwear empower kids and help them fit in with their peers.

You can find stylish adaptive clothing and shoes on websites like Etsy and Zappos and at Billy Footwear, Target, JCPenney, Kohl's, Seven7 Jeans, Tommy Hilfiger, and many more retailers. Skechers slip-in shoes, a great find, are Noni's go-to favorites.

When my two youngest came home from middle school with a story about a classmate with intellectual disabilities who didn't have any nice clothes, my ears perked up, because appearance matters. He may have looked a bit scruffy, but my kids took a liking to Jatinder and wanted to help.

Kids with disabilities are cool, and it helps to dress the part.

"He's an awesome kid, Mom, but he really needs clothes, so we're going to give him some of ours," they said. They headed for their dresser drawers and reappeared ready to part with a small stack of shirts, shorts, and jeans.

The good deed caught on when a bunch of their friends decided to pitch in too. In no time, Jatinder had a complete school wardrobe. Almost.

"Mom, Jatinder still needs a few things, and the only way we can get them is to buy them at the store," they determined. "He needs a belt so his pants don't fall down, because he's skinny. He needs a pair of khakis so he can dress up for assemblies. And a jogging suit would be sweet."

"I'm willing to take you to the store," I said, "if you're willing to contribute some of your own money." They handed over ten bucks each.

Because they cared about him, a group of typical kids transformed the middle-school experience for one friend with developmental disabilities. For their kindness, they got to see Jatinder sporting his new duds each day, walking on air.

The hunt for cool clothes intensifies as kids with disabilities become adults. When it's time to be fancy for a special occasion, like a wedding, high-heeled shoes and strapless dresses aren't options for Noni. Think broken ankle or clothing malfunction.

We stick with cute flats. But sometimes even flats won't do as the night winds down and her dancing feet have had enough. "Here," she says as she tosses her shoes my way, "I'm done with these. And these too." She pulls out hairpins, sending her updo into a downward spiral.

She can be a waif when she wants to.

"I don't think she'll ever date." (Ha!)

My husband and I nearly choked when we heard those words expressed by a well-meaning relative at a family gathering when our daughter was 4 years old. Dating? She was barely toddling.

I hadn't thought that far ahead. But the speculation, spoken aloud, broke a little piece of my heart. I wasn't in denial, but I also wasn't ready to give up the possibility, either.

Then along came Todd, the cutest darn boy in fourth grade and Noni's first "crush." At the lunch table in the cafeteria one day, the little girls took turns revealing which boy they liked, and she picked the kindest one.

Years later, Todd is still sweet to her, and his wife, Jackie, delights in telling the story of Noni as his first love.

Among school-aged children, nearly twice as many boys have developmental disabilities compared with girls.

According to the U.S. Centers for Disease Control and Prevention, the prevalence is higher in boys, at 10.76 percent, than girls, at 5.31 percent.

Lucky Noni had her pick of boys and went to more high-school dances than any of her siblings! Her escorts would tell you she was The. Best. Date. Ever. Because she dances the night away. With everybody. She once joined in her sister's slow dance at prom, making it a threesome and making everyone smile.

Proms and homecomings would typically start with a reception at our home for the whole group of friends with special needs and their dates. These "just friends" would gather around the piano singing at the top of their lungs while Gregory, with musical talents and Down syndrome, played his repertoire of church hymns! For the parents, the scene was an alleluia moment.

One year, Noni's date for her senior prom was her friend Seth from a neighboring high school. What a good-looking couple they made. Tall and athletic with a rare genetic disorder known as cri du chat syndrome, or cat's cry, Seth was especially excited for post-prom at the rec center, where he headed straight for the popular climbing wall, determined to reach the top.

After multiple attempts to scale the wall, he made little progress but showed no sign of giving up. The line of eager teens awaiting their turn was growing. Most didn't know Seth since he went to a different school.

All eyes fell on his mom. "Don't look at me," said Peggy. "I'm not going to tell him he can't do it."

Neither would anyone else. One by one, four dads came to the rescue, gripping Seth's safety harness and using all their might to help hoist him to the top, with a chorus of teens chanting, "Seth! Seth! Seth!"

You guessed it. With a little help from his new friends, he reached the summit and smacked the buzzer, elated. The teen-packed place erupted in cheers.

Proof positive that inclusion lifts us all up.

What if my child never reads?

I broached this haunting question with Noni's first-grade teacher. Her answer: "Well, lots of people can't read and most don't have her excuse. They learn to compensate, and she will too if she never learns to read."

Never learns to read? Unfathomable to me.

I love to read. Reading is the key to learning. Reading opens a whole world of possibilities to us. Reading is joyful. In our family, it's mandatory. Come hell or high water, my kid was gonna learn to read!

Reading became a top goal at school. Day after day, year after year, committed teachers, tutors, and family did their best. We tried every known method and even made up a few.

It never happened. One of my deepest fears came to be. Noni cannot read. She cannot decipher letters, words, or numbers.

And that's okay, I learned.

Like others who cannot read, she *has* learned to compensate. She recognizes many words as visuals. She knows her cereals, restaurants, stores, and road signs.

When she sees french fries on the menu, she wants 'em. She knows her first name when she sees it and can pick out mail addressed to her.

Only when we let go of everything we knew about learning to read and began to think about reading in a new way did we land on a pleasing compromise.

Midway through high school, we changed Noni's goal from learning to read to learning to love books. Just like reading in the beanbag chairs with classmates in middle school, she had helpers in her teen years. Each day, a student volunteered to give up a study hall to spend time with her in the media center, paging through books and magazines popular with teens.

Noni became hooked.

Today, she enjoys leafing through coffee-table books, magazines, photo albums, and, her personal favorite, dictionaries with pictures and razor-thin pages that feel good. She's given new definition to the concept of reading.

It works for her and for Mom too.

"OPTIMISMS" TO LIVE BY

KIDS WITH disabilities yearn to feel a sense of belonging, just like everybody else. Give them that joy, bask in it yourself, and share it with everybody. Speak up. Classrooms, play groups, ball fields, cheer teams, libraries, art classes, music lessons, and workplaces are open for everyone's participation. We're living in the age of inclusion.

Gifted and Talented? You Bet!

*Everyone has something to contribute, and
everyone deserves a chance to shine.*
EUNICE KENNEDY SHRIVER, founder of Special Olympics

E UNICE KENNEDY SHRIVER, a champion of individuals with intellectual disabilities, founded Special Olympics in 1968 in Chicago, where some 1,000 athletes from the United States and Canada competed in the first games.

In 1977, at the opening ceremonies of the International Summer Games in South Bend, Indiana, she gave this famous charge to the Special Olympians:

You are the stars and the world is watching you. By your presence, you send a message to every village, every city, every nation. A message of hope. A message of victory.
The right to play on any playing field? You have earned it.
The right to study in any school? You have earned it.
The right to hold a job? You have earned it.
The right to be anyone's neighbor? You have earned it.

It took guts to carry the torch for kids and adults like ours in an unenlightened era in the 1960s. For the love of her own sister with intellectual disabilities, Shriver stood up for the rights of this slighted population. She showed the world their capabilities and worth and defied conventional notions of the day.

She ignited a can-do spirit that continues to light the way for our children and for future generations.

Handicaps schmandicaps!

When you take off the training wheels and feel the thrill of riding free, it's official: You're a big kid now.

Noni's little sister was almost 5 years old, itching to learn to ride her bike one spring. Off came the training wheels and out came Mommy and Daddy taking turns blocking, tackling, and catching Jacy before she tipped over.

Someone else watching was not happy about it. "I want my training wheels off too," Noni whined, pouting. She hated to see her younger sister doing something she wanted to do but couldn't.

Without a second thought, Daddy said, "Hey, she wants her training wheels off? I'm not telling her no. Are you? Okay then, I'll take them off for now and put them back on later."

Off they came, and off she went. Pedaling her two-wheeler all by herself! Who knew years of riding on training wheels back and forth on the sidewalk thousands of times had propelled our 8-year-old with enough practice to ride a two-wheeler?

Everything in her diagnosis, which includes a neurodevelopmental coordination disorder known as dyspraxia, indicated she wasn't supposed to be able to do this. Dyspraxia, a partial loss of motor skills, makes her, for the most part, unable to plan and coordinate large and small muscle groups.

Occupational and physical therapies were helping improve her balance, coordination, and leg strength. But being able to bike ride? Unimaginable for this kid.

Standing in my suburban cul-de-sac witnessing a miracle, I was joined by neighbors who came out to see Noni ride. Between excitement, laughter, and tears, I told my neighbor I never thought I'd see this day.

"Shame on you, Mom," she replied. "Don't ever put limits on her."

I, the mom who prides herself in being progressive and raising this child to live life fully, had underestimated her—and the power of practice.

When motor skills are a struggle for your child, practice is the best teacher. Not just ordinary practice, but extraordinary repetition. Not ten times, but ten thousand times. That's how much work she put into learning to ride a bike. We do whatever it takes.

For "Show Off Your Talent Day" at school, we were so excited because she had achieved something big to share. As her inclusion classmates gathered in the school yard, Noni hopped on her thick-wheeled, bright-turquoise Hampton Cruiser and put on a performance, beaming proudly to their cheering and clapping. They all knew this big-kid moment for her was a big deal.

Afterward, a typical classmate approached her. "I wish I could ride a bike like you, Noni," she said. "I'm still learning."

We're still learning, too, to let our girl fly.

Cool tech for cool kids

"I'm one of those never-give-up moms," says Elaine. "I wasn't ready to give up snow skiing just because Alana has disabilities. So I found a way."

The solution for Alana, with rare HUWEI gene disorder, has been attending the Phoenix Adaptive Ski Program at HoliMont Ski Resort in Ellicottville, New York, one of a growing number of adaptive programs for children and adults throughout North America and Europe.

Thanks to leaps and bounds in technology and shifts in attitudes, the world of adaptive skiing is making the magic of the mountains accessible for an increasing number of skiers and boarders, according to Matt Masson, in the winter sports 2020 guide in *National Geographic Traveller* (UK).

Audrey's mother, Tara, remembers doctors predicting her daughter with CASK gene disorder would "never walk, talk, or be a ballerina." Unfathomable insensitivity.

Proving doctors so wrong and pushing limits, Amazing Audrey became a surfer instead.

Incredible equipment—including specialized snow skis, surfboards, water skis, paddleboards tricked out with seats, outriggers, tethers, handles, and more—make once-unthinkable sports possible for people with developmental and physical disabilities.

Families also find it tough to take a child with limited mobility on hikes, nature trails, or simply a walk in the park. Innovative technology is making the outdoors more reachable with accessibility carts like the Huckleberry Cascade Cart, jogging strollers like the Special Tomato Jogger, and lots and lots of adapted bikes and trikes.

Not surprising to parents, such specialized equipment is often expensive. Welcome to the world of raising kids with disabilities.

Katie Bergeron Peglow started the Adaptivemall.com to help families explore new devices to give their children every possible opportunity. The site is filled with a variety of specialized gear to help with sitting, standing, walking, bathing, eating, traveling, and having fun.

Peglow, a physical therapist, was inspired to start the Adaptivemall.com by growing up with Carrie, her younger sister with Down syndrome. This experience gave Peglow insight into the challenges and rewards that come with special needs. "My goal," she says, "is to empower parents with resources."

Parents like Elaine and Scott. They introduced Alana to the slopes at age 6, starting on a magic carpet attached to her teachers on a beginner-level ski run. Today at 16, this young lady with multiple disabilities has progressed to ski lift and independent skiing accompanied by her guides.

Mom beams when she talks about her daughter's skiing. "She doesn't care if it's freezing, snowing, or raining. She's out every possible weekend," Elaine bragged. "I could watch her all day!"

When the snow melts, Alana, who likes to be active, will reach for her bike and her bathing suit, getting ready for the next season of outdoor activities. She's a girl who's nonverbal and needs help with most everything, but she bikes, swims, and skis! She's unstoppable!

Parents who encourage kids to reach for the stars or the mountains embolden them with can-do attitudes.

Bowling alleys ahead of the curve

Long before adaptive sports became mainstream, bowling alleys led the way, welcoming and accommodating those with disabilities. If there's one activity wildly popular with throngs of individuals with disabilities, it's bowling.

If the sport is looking for an ambassador, look no further than Billy, a young adult with developmental disabilities and on the autism spectrum, who can't get enough of it. He loves to bowl and, with an average of 180, he's good at it.

In Billy's world, if it's Wednesday, he's bowling with friends Greg, Kim, and Noni. If it's Sunday, he's league bowling with Mom and Dad, Marianne and Bill. If it's Special Olympics, he's bowling against seasoned competitors for medals and pride.

Why is bowling so popular? It's a social sport relatively easy to learn and play. No expensive equipment required, just a pair of shoes and a ball, and you're ready to roll.

For more than forty years, Friends Forever, a Cleveland, Ohio nonprofit, has made it possible for individuals with all kinds of disabilities to bowl nine months of the year and participate in tournaments and banquets. On any given Saturday, picture the lanes filled with more than a hundred bowlers with all sorts of special needs having a ball!

A variety of adaptive equipment opens the sport to these individuals. Ball ramps, ball pushers, lightweight balls, gutter bumpers, guide rails, and wheelchair apparatus help bowlers aim for the pins.

Thanks to the adaptability of this sport, those who are intellectually and physically limited have the chance to enjoy its cognitive, physical, and social benefits alongside their friends and family.

Noni has invented her own adaptation. Since learning to bowl as a youngster, she put into play her unconventional form—bowling overhand. For her, unlearning overhand or relearning underhand is not an option. No dissuading her. She's adamant, "I'm right."

She launches her ball overhand down the lane with a loud thud. We've only been asked to leave a bowling alley one time. Her novel approach also saves us the cost of drilling holes into her bowling ball. Because who needs 'em?

Little brother Trent copied Noni's form as a third-grader and won the school's best-bowler-of-the-year trophy. Now, her 3- and 5-year-old nieces, Charlotte and Camryn, are picking up Noni's signature move.

On the rarest of occasions, Noni beats Billy on a Wednesday afternoon, and Billy is not happy. He must have bowled an off game precisely when she miraculously managed to get a couple of strikes and spares.

Billy lets it roll like the good sport he is, ready with a high five for his longtime friend who's tickled by her lucky win. She did it!

With a thud.

Little Miss Sunshine

The stage is Eve's happy place.

She won the Ohio Miss Amazing pageant and competed in Nashville, Tennessee, for the national title, showcasing her abilities, confidence, and personality.

She auditioned and landed a spot on the Cleveland Cavaliers No Limits dance team, an enthusiastic group of performers with special needs who display their talents and spread joy at Cavs home games. It's the first and only dance team in the NBA for those with special needs.

In high school, she lettered in varsity cheerleading and dance team. She went to every homecoming dance all dressed up, on the arm of her boyfriend, who also has Down syndrome.

Eve is nailing her goal to be a rock star, but her extraordinary accomplishments are far from what experts predicted.

The doctor gave Eve's mom, Maria, the "bad" news over the phone. Her unborn baby girl had Down syndrome. The "good" news? "You still have time to terminate the pregnancy," he told her. The year was 2004, not that long ago.

Maria was awash in tears that wouldn't stop. She and her husband, Dan, knew little about Down syndrome and now needed to know everything, so they went to see a geneticist.

"You need to terminate this pregnancy," they were advised. The geneticist listed all the reasons why as Maria bawled:

- Society won't accept her.
- You won't be able to bond with her.
- She will be an outcast.
- She will be a burden.
- She will have a depressing life.
- Her sisters will resent her.
- Your family will be a sad one.
- You're going to lose all your friends.
- You will end up divorced.

So Dan did what Dan does. He slammed his fist on the desk and shouted, "Don't say those things to my wife. That's it. We're outta here!" He took Maria's hand and stormed out, launching a few choice words of warning into the flabbergasted waiting room.

Eve was born two months premature and underwent her first surgery the day after birth. She went through several more within the first four months of her life for heart, airway, and intestinal problems. She was fed through a mic-key button, or G-tube, until she began learning to eat solid food around age 4 with the help of a feeding clinic. Hers was a rough start.

Going to school was a high point for Eve and Mom. "Her preschool teacher, Miss Brizius, influenced me so much because she believed in Eve," Maria explained. "She made sure Eve got all the supports and resources she needed to be successful as an inclusion student."

The value of having an excellent teacher early on is immeasurable. Parents learn from creative and caring teachers like Miss Brizius what their child needs and how to advocate for them all through their school years. As a result, Eve loves school and learning, and the students love her.

Her classmates spoil her. They buy her ice cream, tie her shoes for her even though she can do it herself, and let her cut in line. "Stop!" says Maria. "Now she's trying to sneak ahead in line at the grocery store!"

When the dance-team coach said she really wanted Eve on the team and she didn't have to try out, Maria said absolutely not. "She has to work for it. She needs the discipline expected of everyone else. She doesn't need things handed to her. Trying out will give her confidence."

She tried out. She made the team.

At 20, Eve takes part in the school's job training program, building employment and life skills at various businesses in the community. She is learning how to shop, prepare food, recycle, clean, and more.

"She hates cleaning," Maria laughed. "It's not likely to be her chosen career path."

Down syndrome proved to be one dimension of Eve. Another is being audacious!

At home she's expected to keep her room tidy, put her laundry away, and empty the dishwasher, Maria explains. "When she empties the dishwasher, you can hear her mumble, 'This is unfair. This is bullshit!'"

So were those early prognoses.

Today, this family's bonds are strong. Maria and Dan celebrated their twenty-fifth wedding anniversary. Their friends are many. Eve and her two older sisters are besties. Eve is working hard and living a joyful life with her happy family in her accepting community.

Down syndrome proved to be one dimension of Eve. Another is being audacious!

How could doctors have been so wrong?

Isn't it about time the medical community abandons obsolete thinking and catches up with the human potential of people born with Down syndrome? There's so much to know about this condition and others that can't be found in medical journals. Instead, doctors stand to learn a lot from families like Eve's.

Because she and others with Down syndrome are finding their place in the sun.

Try a little tenderness

Kevin, a storied college quarterback, came up short in the national championship game. He was crestfallen. Afterward, at a somber gathering of family and friends that should have been a celebration, he sat silent and dejected. Everybody knew instinctively to give him space.

Except Noni. She bolted his way, squeezed in right next to him, and began rubbing his back.

"Aww, Kevin," she comforted her cousin, inching closer, laying her head on his shoulder. "Aww, Kev," she said as she swayed, running her fingers through his hair. No prodding would budge her.

"I hate to admit it," Kevin broke the silence, "but this actually feels good."

A moment of affection bonded two incomparable cousins, both gifted, one in athletics, the other in empathy. In this setting, she was the only one to breach his orbit, with her innocent tenderness and pure love, just what he needed.

According to author Dr. Jacqueline Acho in her book *Currency of Empathy,* affective empathy develops in infancy. Our earliest memories are "feeling" memories.

"Did you know picking up yawns is a reflection of empathy?" asks Acho. "It's one of the most primitive forms of embodied empathy."

Our daughter may struggle with cognitive and motor skills, but she's got empathy down pat. Yawn and she'll yawn too. Her siblings purposely yawn in front of her, and when she automatically yawns back, they roar with laughter. "Gotcha!"

She watches the news and feels bad when someone is injured in a car crash or fire. "Oh no, someone got hurt. Please pray, everybody."

She loves the Weather Channel but winces when she hears about tornadoes or hurricanes. "Watch out, people. Be careful. Please."

On the other extreme, she literally jumps with joy for *Wheel of Fortune* contestants who solve puzzles and win fabulous trips. "She's going to Greece! Oh, yeah!"

She claps through *The Price is Right*, *Let's Make a Deal*, and *Jeopardy!* because she is always excited for winners. *Everybody Loves Raymond*, too, but nobody loves him like Noni.

She waves and cheers on her competitors in Special Olympics, even as they pass her on the cycling course.

If you're happy, she's happy. If you're blue, she senses it too.

You feel the warmth of her empathy when it rubs off on you.

Just ask Kevin.

Autism does indeed speak

Who is Talia? After twenty-four years of silence, her parents, Lisa and Rob, are getting to know their daughter for the first time. She's found her "voice" after being nonverbal for most of her life.

At 3 years old, Talia was diagnosed with autism. Her inability to speak and express herself led to regular outbursts of screaming, kicking, and biting. High levels of frustration rippled through the family and became their way of life. Her parents tried everything, and then some.

Recently, a friend urged Lisa to read the book *Underestimated* by father and son J.B. Handley and Jamison Handley. It's a remarkable story of J.B.'s teenage son with autism, Jamison, who was able to unlock his thoughts using a novel communication method, Spelling to Communicate, or S2C, pioneered by the International Association for Spelling as Communication.

Lisa was a skeptic. Leery and weary. Her friend, however, kept pestering, so to appease the friend, Lisa bought the book. This won't work, she thought but gave it a try anyway, because that's what never-give-up parents do.

Thank goodness she did, because it worked for Talia! "It's changed our lives," Lisa exclaimed.

The fresh theory behind S2C is that nonspeaking kids diagnosed with autism are presumed competent but cannot make their bodies do what they want or need them to do. The disability is not in cognition but in motor planning and execution, a condition known as apraxia, a severe loss of motor functions.

Small-motor skills involved in speech are highly complex, among the finest of the fine motors, making it extremely hard for kids with apraxia to use their mouths to talk or their fingers to write or type. S2C works around this disability. Individuals poke at letters on a letterboard, exerting their whole arm, shoulder, and upper body and using large-motor muscles, movements easier for them.

By pointing this way, Talia can spell words and sentences to transmit what she is thinking, releasing her language within, freeing her to "speak" her mind.

Speech-language pathologist Elizabeth Vosseller of the Growing Kids Therapy Center in Herndon, Virginia, is the founder of the S2C method now practiced by a growing number of trained professionals and clinics. The success of thousands of individuals using S2C fortifies her premise: Language is cognitive. Speech is motor.

S2C has changed the narrative and challenged conventional wisdom in the autism field, causing controversy, particularly among advocates of Applied Behavior Analysis, the longstanding gold-standard therapy for autism. Both methods have their critics and proponents.

Talia's mom, Lisa, once a skeptic of S2C, is now a convert. "It's a miracle," she exuded. "There's no other way to describe the transformation in my daughter. It's changed her life and ours for the better in every way."

"We never knew how sophisticated and smart she was," Lisa continued. "All her life, she heard everything and absorbed more than anyone ever imagined. But she was trapped in silence, treated in school as if she had intellectual disabilities when she didn't. Imagine her frustration! No wonder she had behavioral issues."

Today, Talia is happier than ever before and immensely proud of herself. In one of her first messages to her mom, she spelled, "Thank you, Mom, for never giving up on me." At that, the floodgates opened wide, with Lisa awash in tears.

These parents are learning a lot about their daughter now. Her favorite color is red. They never knew. When they asked where she'd like to go on vacation, she spelled, "snow-covered mountains." A family train trip through Canada made her wish come true.

"My voice is quiet and my mind is loud.
Nonspeakers are not nonthinkers."

When asked what makes her feel joy, Talia responded, "Healing my mental health by spelling to communicate." She is forming aspirations for the first time in her life. "Being part of this revolution is a gift. I would love to tell my story to the world in hopes of reaching many nonspeakers like me."

After so much time being unable to communicate, the complex sentences Talia is now using to express her knowledge, thoughts, and feelings is astounding.

When asked for the meaning of the word "genre," she answered: "A genre is a category of music, movies, TV shows, or books. Reality and drama are two of my favorites."

Prompted to describe something else you can do on a smartphone besides listening to music, she responded: "One can watch shows, play games, search the web, scroll through social media, read books, take photos, send emails, and communicate with family and friends."

What should people know and understand about Talia? In her words, "I am brilliant. I am listening. I am loving and gentle. My voice is quiet and my mind is loud. Nonspeakers are not nonthinkers."

Talia and her parents are at the beginning of this exciting foray into words, thoughts, and desires. Awestruck, they are rewriting a future of possibilities.

"Nothing," says Talia, "compares to being understood."

"OPTIMISMS" TO LIVE BY

EVERYBODY IS good at something and not so good at something else. Disabilities force us to focus our energies on our kids' strengths. Involve them in activities where they can shine. Watch them beam with pride in their abilities and work hard to get even better. Then prepare to stand in awe of them.

This Life Is Difficult

You are so brave and quiet I forget you are suffering.
ERNEST HEMINGWAY, American novelist, *A Farewell to Arms*

EVERY PARENT of a child with developmental disabilities, like autism, yearns to crawl inside their child's mind and body for a glimpse of what they think and feel. If only it were possible.

I often develop my empathy through reading good books, Hemingway's and others. A favorite of mine is *Love Anthony* by contemporary fiction author Lisa Genova, whose books are inspired by neuroscience and who takes us inside the thoughts of her character Anthony, a young boy with autism.

My brain is made up of different rooms... If I'm counting the square tiles on the kitchen floor (180), I'm in my Numbers Room, but if my mother starts talking to me, I have to go into my Ears Room to hear her. But I want to stay in Numbers because I'm counting, and I like to count, but my mother keeps talking... then she grabs my hand and this surprises me and forces me into Hands, which isn't where I want to go... and she's talking to me but I can't hear what she's saying because I'm in my Hands Room and not in Ears...

She's saying, "Look at me." But if I look at her, I have to leave Ears and go into Eyes, and then I won't be able to hear what she's saying. So I don't know what to do... and I can't make a decision on where to go, and I'm In Between, and that's when I get into trouble.

Imagine that.

Emily's son, Henry, with autism, is sensitive to sound, which makes it nearly impossible for the family to go to restaurants. He'll scream bloody murder if he hears the slightest bit of clapping, whether from live-track music or nearby birthday celebrations. While Mom and Dad grasp what's happening, few restaurant patrons do.

Novels like Genova's *Love Anthony* and Mark Haddon's delightful tale *The Curious Incident of the Dog in the Night-Time* can help us better understand intractable conditions that wreak havoc.

Above all, they lead us to have deeper compassion for individuals and families whose lives, for all kinds of reasons, are difficult.

Careless words cut deep

Lots of kids need braces. In our house, all of them did. When it was Noni's turn, the orthodontist said, "You'll have to decide if it's worth it."

Sometimes you need to fire back at professionals. Or fire them.

Call me supersensitive; most moms like me are. Those words, code for "if *she's* worth it," stung.

Blood boiling, I snapped back, "Why would I invest in braces for my other kids but not for her? Give me one good reason."

Silence.

For my money and the prospect of giving our girl a pretty smile, we need more than a technically competent doctor. We need an enlightened one. You'd be surprised what comes out of the mouths of professionals. Sometimes you need to fire back at them. Or fire them.

Here are some true stories from our experience:

Neurologist: "You're familiar with a bell curve? Your daughter is probably here on the curve," he said, pointing off the curve to nowhere.

Me: "I think we're done here. C'mon, sweetie, it's time to go home." And never come back.

Newly minted physical therapist at elementary school conference: "Do you realize your daughter needs help? A *lot* of help!"

Me: "Yes, I am her mother and I do not live under a rock. Furthermore, be careful what you say to me. Keep in mind I love her." I found these words of caution to be a good way to start every IEP meeting!

Adapted sports coach: "I don't think your daughter fits in our baseball program. She isn't able to throw a ball or swing a bat, and she doesn't seem to like getting dirty."

Me: "I'm glad you're having this conversation with me, because I'll make sure you never tell another family their child with special needs doesn't fit into a special-needs program."

Did I just say that?

When I was a young mom, careless word choices could reduce me to tears, especially coming from the credentialed. The voices in our heads can masterfully plant self-doubts:

- Do they know better than me what's best for her?
- Are they right?
- Am I in denial?

Over time, though, fighting back tears gives way to fighting back. When being nice doesn't get you anywhere, getting pissed often does. It can ignite your courage. Think Popeye downing a can of spinach. Or Superman stepping out of a phone booth.

Deep within yourself, you find your steel. You transform into a formidable force for your child and stand up to the insensitivity of authorities and professionals.

They may know a lot, but they don't know it all.

Deep within, you find your steel. You transform into a formidable force for your child.

Without words to tell you what hurts

How did this happen?

"I don't know" is a common response of parents whose nonverbal child gets hurt. Spotting an injury can be difficult for parents who don't witness it happen.

Minimally mobile and nonverbal, 10-year-old Melody, with CASK gene disorder, appeared to be in pain. Sensing something was wrong, Mom Karen took her to the hospital—twice. With little to go on and hundreds of possibilities, doctors poked, prodded, pulled, and pushed. Frustrated by her inability to pinpoint precisely where she was hurting, doctors sent Melody home, only to have her return again.

This time, more testing revealed a fractured knee, a surprise to everyone. Since Mom couldn't explain how it happened, social services was called to pay a home visit, adding insult to injury.

Similarly, 4-year-old Sarah, another child with a CASK disorder, entered the hospital in distress, seemingly having spasms. Sarah couldn't tell her family or the doctors where it hurt. It took several days of testing for myriad potential causes before doctors discovered she had a broken leg.

How does a youngster in a wheelchair break her leg? Mom Laura didn't know. School officials didn't know. England's safeguarding team was called in to investigate.

The finding: Limited ability to walk weakens bones and increases the chances of fractures, a side effect of being in a wheelchair. Sarah's fracture likely occurred not by trauma but on its own.

When young Charlotte's frequent bruising triggered the safeguarding team to investigate, they found no fault with her parents' care. For days, however, the parents were presumed guilty of child abuse, and the trauma caused Mom Jane to suffer a mental health crisis.

Clumsiness, too, can send kids with disabilities to the hospital recurrently. Trips and falls come with Noni's motor deficits. Though she has words, she has difficulty isolating and communicating which part of her body hurts.

When she was a youngster, I joked we might need to find another emergency room because our many visits were beginning to raise more questions, a notion not farfetched.

When she obliviously walked into the path of her brother swinging a wooden baseball bat (concussion), jumped off a picnic table (broken foot), and fell on her face umpteen times (stitches and chipped teeth), this mom had a lot of explaining to do, because Noni couldn't.

She walked around for a day on a broken foot before we realized something was wrong, and we felt like terrible parents.

We can all agree society needs safeguards to protect the well-being of children and adults with disabilities because they are at higher risk for abuse and neglect. But the best of parents can find themselves in a precarious situation when a child with disabilities is injured and can't answer the question "What happened?"

Mom and Dad shudder when they don't know the answer either.

Appearances can be deceiving

In a flash, the whirly toy in Noni's hand wound up in the picture-perfect golden locks of the little girl standing beside her in the toy store, twisting her long blond curls into a gnarly bird nest.

With shock and horror, the girl's grandma pounced.

"How dare you!" she shouted at my 5-year-old. "Look what you've done! That was not nice! You should be ashamed!"

You get the picture.

In the chaos, I collected my brood of four and tried to calm Noni, who was frightened and wailing. With a bluster, Grandma plopped her oversized pocketbook and wad of keys into my already full arms. "Here," she barked. "The least you can do is hold these while I try to untangle this mess."

On my knees facing my distraught daughter, I tried to explain the consequences of her innocent actions. Knowing she couldn't quite understand, I reassured her: "It was an accident; you didn't mean it; you're sorry, and we can fix it."

I wiped the tears and snot from her face, and she quieted down as her young siblings tried to make her feel better, each chiming in, "It's okay, Noni."

Suddenly, Grandma, who'd been listening, stopped her frenzy, going quiet and pale.

"*Oh!*" she gasped, "I am *so* sorry. I didn't understand. But I do now. Please forgive me."

I do. I'm sorry too.

"Let me help you untangle this mess," I offered, and she let me help.

Having a child whose disabilities at first glance may be invisible, I can be forgiving of people's comments, but it's not always easy.

I admit to yelling at a geezer who challenged me when I parked in a disability space. I was treating my young kids to lunch at a little neighborhood restaurant and used a handicap spot because it was snowing. Wiping out on snow and ice is in Noni's DNA, especially when my hands were full carrying her baby brother. I use disability parking only when we need it. In that situation, we did.

Suddenly, an older gentleman rolled down his window to scold me for having no handicap and no business parking there. I was steaming in the cold. I settled the kids inside the eatery, then stepped outside for a moment to unleash on him.

"Things are not always as they seem," I snapped. "In case you didn't notice, I have a daughter with disabilities. My life is hard enough without you adding your two cents."

Not my proudest moment, though venting felt cathartic, and it got the message across to him, albeit harshly. What I should have added, nicely, was "I forgive you."

It's easy to jump to the wrong conclusion. We all do it. But if you look through empathetic eyes, you may be struck by something invisible:

- Is the youngster having a meltdown a spoiled brat? Or does he have autism?
- Is the neighbor becoming a grouch? Or is dementia setting in?
- Is the unsteady lady drunk? Or recovering from a stroke?
- Is the little girl getting out of her wheelchair faking? Or learning to walk?

Take a second look.

To work or not to work?

If only childcare weren't so expensive in America. For most families, moving to Iceland, Norway, Sweden, Denmark, or Finland for the world's best childcare isn't an option.

As bad as the problem is for all parents with young children, it's even worse for families of children with special needs. They are three times more likely to experience job disruptions compared with other parents, most often because of childcare problems, according to data from the U.S. National Survey of Children's Health.

Cost and quality are the biggest obstacles. In the majority of states in America, it's more expensive to send a child to daycare for a year than to an in-state public university. For kids with disabilities, the cost is greater, and the need for high-quality care, greater yet. What's a family to do?

Researchers found in nearly 15 percent of these families, at least one parent scaled back or stopped working because of a child's condition. That figure jumps to more than 40 percent in families of children with intellectual disabilities, the singular commonality shared by nearly every child you read about in this book. To no one's surprise, women shoulder a disproportionate share of caregiving, work interruptions, and career sacrifices.

American families reducing work hours or leaving jobs to care for their children with special needs lose an average of $18,000 in annual income, according to an analysis published in the journal *Pediatrics* in 2021. What sacrifices they make for love of a child! How much more can we pile on parents of children with special needs before they crack? Theirs is already a crushing load.

To work or not to work? There's no right or wrong answer.

I agonized over what to do before making my decision to become a stay-at-home mom to my four kids when they were young. Our family balance was tipping out of control and needed righting.

The upside of putting my career on hold? Time. To devote to Noni's considerable needs. To spend with my only-little-once kids. The downside? My own best interests would take a back seat.

I worried. Was this move to leave the workplace career suicide for me? In moments of panic, I would tell myself, "If you were good once, you can be good again!" That morale booster kept me going, especially on days I felt I was losing myself as I was caring for everybody else.

For me, staying home was the hardest job ever.

One morning, my husband phoned and asked what I was doing. I went off on him. "I'm so glad you asked," I raised my voice. "I'm chiseling dried-on scrambled eggs off the baby's high-chair tray. Honing my chiseling skills, that's what I'm doing. It's an enriching, growing professional-development experience, and I'm becoming a master chiseler!"

"Honey, how 'bout I call you later?" Good idea.

I stayed home for nearly four years, until our savings dwindled and my desire to return to work intensified.

I eased in and escaped back to work gradually over a few years, increasing from three to four to five days a week once my two youngest were in preschool. We were lucky to find quality care for four kids, but it cost us a fortune. For most families, the need for childcare diminishes as kids grow up. But for families like ours, it never does.

It may get easier as time goes by, but it never ends.

It's an emergency! Um, never mind.

The human tendency to protect and overprotect those with disabilities is understandable, but sometimes we go too far. It happens in school, a lot.

I'd get calls from well-meaning school officials letting me know Noni's nose was running. "Wipe it with a tissue from the box I sent in at the start of the school year," I'd suggest.

"Will you be coming to get her?" was the next predictable question. Please don't lay that guilt trip on me. I am working, and she is fine.

No one called when my other kids had runny noses.

When she fell on the playground one day, I got the call at work that her wrist was hurting. "Did you ask her if her wrist was hurting?" I inquire. Of course they did, and she said yes to the leading suggestion.

"Is it broken?" I ask. "No? Then tell her to shake it off. She's perfectly fine to go back to class and take the bus home."

I'm used to telling Noni to shake it off. After bumping her elbow or stubbing her toe, this lighthearted reassurance helps still the quivering bottom lip and stave off the tears about to spill over practically nothing.

In my favorite call from school about nothing, I was told Noni had an eye infection, which got my attention. "Are you sure it's an eye infection and not the mosquito bite on her cheek?"

Concerned, I headed from work to school to find nothing more than a mosquito bite. "Will you be taking her home?" I was asked. No, I will be heading back downtown to work, guilt free.

Likewise, Kristina was frustrated by repeated calls from school when her daughter Eliana, with CASK gene disorder, was complaining of pain. She knew Eliana was faking, again. Yes, just like typical kids, ours can be clever when they want attention or to break free from class.

Fed up, Kristina heeded the call, headed to school, but refused to take her child home. Instead, she sat in the office helping her daughter complete schoolwork. Staff thought Mom was heartless until Eliana's nonsensical complaints escalated: "Knees are bwoken! Knees on fire! Neeeed a trampoline!"

When Karen's daughter Ashley, with developmental disabilities, started her period, Mom received a call informing her Ashley could not attend school during her menstrual cycle. She was to stay home that week. Is this a school policy for all girls? Nope, strictly an Ashley policy.

Distraught, Mom wondered, Can they do that? Hell no!

Recognizing an egregious violation of her daughter's right to equal access for learning in the classroom, Karen marched up to school to read them the riot act—and send Ashley back to class.

False alarms create chaos for busy parents of students with special needs. Runny noses, bumps and bruises, periods, and faking it are easily remedied with tissues, bandages, pads, or reassurances.

Get back to class, Henny Penny, Goosey Loosey, Ducky Lucky, Turkey Lurkey, and Chicken Little, because the sky is not falling.

Good parents can have kids with bad behaviors

Robby is a gentle teddy bear most of the time, especially in his favorite sensory spaces, awash in calming sounds and lights, soft mats, and an air swing hanging from the ceiling.

Triggers and sensory overload, however, can send him raging. His multiple diagnoses of autism, psychosis, attention deficit hyperactivity disorder, and profound intellectual disability combine to produce extreme behaviors.

His super single-mom, Barb, is proud to take her handsome young man, always well groomed and nicely dressed, out in the community. She is highly practiced in de-escalating techniques and therapeutic interventions in the event of an outburst. She is not immune, however, to the passing judgment and social shaming of onlookers.

"You should never bring him out in public," grumbled an elderly woman as Barb escorted Robby out of a restaurant when he became loud.

Over the years, the hardest part for Barb has been losing friends and family. She recalled an intense weekend away visiting family when Robby, as a youngster, jumped into a car, put it in gear, and pretended he was driving. The car rolled down the driveway, across the street, and into the neighbor's house.

He also knocked out window screens and flung neatly manicured yard mulch into the air before Mom could intercept him. "We were never invited back again," she said with regret, "and this was family."

"The stress has taken a toll on my health," she admitted. "I wish more people knew that good parents can indeed have children with behavior disorders."

Emma Nadler, author of *The Unlikely Village of Eden*, can empathize. Her daughter, Eden, born with a rare genetic deletion, is prone to outbursts her older brother has dubbed "fuckfits." Nadler describes being Eden's mother as "both a spiritual calling and something like a fork stuck in my eye."

When you begin to fray, Nadler advises parents to stop trying to do everything alone and learn to share your most precious responsibilities. Barb relies on her village of caregivers for help and respite.

To find strength on those bad days, exasperated moms turn to tried-and-true sources of self-care: Friends, spouses, faith, prayer, exercise, running, walking, nature, music, reading, drawing, meditating, a busy job, a hot shower, humor, chocolate, or a large glass of wine.

Barb can laugh today about young Robby's penchant for communicating by screaming and hollering nonsense. "We finally figured out his shouts of 'Stevie Toony Honey Toony Peepers' meant 'Stephen Spielberg presents *Tiny Toon Adventures*.' In other words, he wanted to watch cartoons!"

He would throw fits for "You likers! You likers! You likers!" Who knew he wanted McDonald's french fries?

As he grew, his behaviors escalated. He became violent and destructive at times. "He could be a danger to himself," Barb said, "and to me, his target. I learned I can't take his behavior personally."

At his worst, he took nine doors off their frames, cracked a bathtub, stomped a hole through the floor and fell into the basement, banged his head through a wall hard enough to knock the outdoor siding off the house, and broke his mother's jaw and ribs.

His uncontrollable outbursts resulted in four hospitalizations for him and a great deal of trial and error working with medical professionals to develop the right chemical balance of psychiatric medications that worked to decrease his outbursts. No such thing as one-size-fits-all.

Today, at 36, Robby lives in a group home just minutes from Mom, who pops in frequently and enjoys taking him out and about. His meds are working, and his quality of life is improving. On the rare occasion when he gets agitated, the intervention of a fast-acting chemical restraint helps calm him.

Challenging behaviors are a known predictor of high stress in parents. My own job of taking care of a child who can't take care of herself is hard work, but not as intensely stressful as Barb's situation.

Parents of children with difficult behaviors have experienced the trauma of protecting their child and themselves from serious injury. They know survival mode and, remarkably, their resilience endures.

Barb and Robby enjoy plenty of good times together, like a recent trip of a lifetime to Disney World. Robby was beyond excited at the thought of riding in an airplane—one of his favorite things—for the first time. Flying in the sky in a real plane made him giddy, which Mom captured in lots of pictures, a moment doubly special because when he's happy, she's happy.

Barb's love for Robby is unconditional.
He is her teddy bear.

Is a miracle on the way?

Raising a child with disabilities is challenging. Battling the ineptitude of government bureaucracy that comes with it is torment.

Here's the outgoing voicemail message of my daughter's Medicaid representative, which apparently is her version of "responsive" customer service: "Hello, this is Mrs. So-and-So, and I'm not available right now. If you already left a message for me, please don't leave another one. All you'll do is fill up my mailbox, and I won't get back to you any sooner."

Then a beep. Then a recording: "This mailbox is full."

Just another day on the merry-go-round of madness.

Who knew the U.S. Social Security Administration is in the business of looking for miracles? About every three years, they investigate individuals with lifelong developmental disabilities to determine if they still have them.

Our daughter? For sure she does. I have mountains of proof.

Imagine my surprise when, upon bureaucratic review, I'm notified my twenty-five pages of required documentation (hard copy, of course) is insufficient. Must be a mistake, I think. Time to call a human for an explanation.

Bureaucrat: "We need more verification to prove her condition has not improved."

Me: "Do you realize," my voice grows louder, "her condition is *permanent*?!"

Bureaucrat: "Yes, but we need to validate she hasn't gotten better."

Me: "Are you familiar with the phrase 'when pigs fly'?"

I remind myself to heed the wise words of American poet Maya Angelou, "Lord, keep Your arm around my shoulder and Your hand over my mouth."

Me: "May I ask why you are checking to see if a disability that doesn't go away has gone away?"

Bureaucrat: "Because it's the rule."

Me: "Do you realize it's a preposterous rule?" The voice in my head admonishes me to Stop. Thinking. Logically.

Bureaucrat: "I don't make the rules, ma'am, I just follow them."

Me: "Your rule is the very definition of insanity. Unless, perhaps, you're on a secret mission to find a miracle, someone cured from a lifetime disability. In that case, I'm all in. Parents like me are always looking for a miracle."

Bureaucrat: "I'm sorry, ma'am."

Me: "Is anyone assessing the intellectual aptitude of the people making up the rules?"

Bureaucrat: "I understand your frustration, ma'am, I really do."

Me: "Hey, I've got an idea, would you like to FaceTime my daughter?"

Bureaucrat: "Pardon me?"

Me: "In less than a minute, you could see for yourself she still has disabilities. Never mind, I already know the answer. I'll snail mail more paperwork."

Weeks later, a second rejection notice arrives. Turns out a lifetime of medical records and school assessments still isn't enough to satisfy paper-pushing doubters.

Next, we are summoned to a mandated appointment with an independent psychologist for a three-hour evaluation. This total stranger will determine if Noni's intellectual disabilities have disappeared, an action beyond insulting to us.

What a colossal waste of time and taxpayer money for a display of government incompetency that eclipses intellectual disability!

Lucky us, we are assigned to a crackerjack psychologist who takes ten minutes, while getting paid for three hours, to corroborate the obvious: "After reviewing the evidence, we find that your disability is continuing."

Dang! We were hoping for a miracle.

"OPTIMISMS" TO LIVE BY

LIVING WITH development disabilities comes with a high degree of difficulty. Just when you think it can't get any harder, something else happens, and it does. But you've proved you can do difficult. You're actually getting good at it. No kidding, give yourself a pat on the back.

Think in New Ways

Grownups suffer from educated incapacity.
EDIE WEINER, leading futurist with the Future Hunters,
author, and keynote speaker

UPON MEETING Edie Weiner at a business conference, I quickly became a follower and she quickly became a friend. She opened my eyes to the baked-in perceptions we all amass over a lifetime that make us incapable of thinking in new ways.

"We call this educated incapacity: Knowing so much about what we already know that we are the last to see the future," said Weiner. "Only through a child's eyes or alien's eyes can you see the world objectively as if you experienced it for the first time. Only then can we get the future right."

I feel a bit like an alien mom every time we approach something new with Noni. Convention doesn't work for my atypical child, but creative thinking often does.

My novel ideas were not always well received by educators and others, causing me to ask, "Why are you looking at me as if I have three heads? Just because you've never done it this way before? Is there a reason we can't give it a try?"

How to see with your heart

What goes through the mind of a young child whose aunt has special needs?

At 4, our grandson Lucas made this observation: "Mommy, when Aunt Jacy babysits Addie and me, she can watch us by herself. When Uncle Trent babysits, he can watch us by himself too. But when Aunt Noni babysits, she has to be with Granny or Papa."

"I think I know why," Lucas surmised. "I think Aunt Noni is the real Wendy, and she lives in Neverland with Peter, and she never grows up. How cool is that!"

In Noni's mind, she didn't come to babysit, she came to play.

Through the eyes of a child, the real Wendy comes to life. Noni as Wendy is a perfect metaphor for my eternal child, suits her to a T. The notion never occurred to me, however, probably because I'm a grown-up bogged down by educated incapacity. The older we get, the more we know, and the harder it is to see differently.

Children, unencumbered by educated incapacity, are free to see what others cannot.

In *The Little Prince*, Antoine de Saint-Exupéry's classic tale, a young alien prince fallen to Earth observes,

The older we get, the more we know, and the harder it is to see differently.

"All grown-ups were once children, though few of them remember it."

Can you see Peter Pan nodding?

I contend parents of kids with special needs qualify as aliens! We've had considerable experience looking through alien eyes.

Our atypical kids are like square pegs trying to fit into round holes, forcing us at every turn to be creative. How many times have I said to myself, "How are we going to make this work for her?"

When young Kevin, with spina bifida, asked for roller skates for his birthday, his mom, Ann, hesitated for a moment. Grandma described his wish as a crazy idea. But Ann replied, "Are you going to tell him no? Because I'm not."

How do you overcome a child's disabilities so he can participate in simple pleasures like roller-skating? When he says with yearning, "I want to do that," you listen. Then you think like Peter Pan.

Ann soon found herself running alongside her birthday boy on his new skates, both of them exhilarated. You get a lot of exercise as a parent, but it keeps you young.

In like fashion, on one of our family vacations, all our kids wanted to parasail. All means all. Noni too. So Daddy rode tandem with her high in the sky.

Plenty of times we eagerly pair up with her for gentle rides on an inflatable tube behind our boat, with her sibs urging Dad to go faster, but he knows better.

We make accommodations when needed. We lift the limbo stick so she can walk under it. We sing along with our Wendy as she belts out "Love Shack" on the karaoke stage.

With a twinkle in your heart, you can conjure up unconventional ways to join in the fun. Sure, lots of people will think you're nuts, but Peter Pan and the Neverland gang will love you for it!

So will your child.

Bring on fun for everyone

When you have young kids, family calendars are packed with activities, too many sometimes. But for kids with special needs, the opposite is true. Pickings are slim and often a long way from home. Proximity matters a lot when you're a child. Where you live is where you make your friends.

What's a parent to do when you can't find neighborhood activities for your child? Here's a suggestion: Do it yourself!

You can start small. Try asking a coach or scout leader, for example, to include your child in an organized activity geared toward typical children. Someone will say yes,

What's a parent to do when you can't find neighborhood activities for your child? Do it yourself!

---

from the heart, and likely make the experience positive for everyone. Find that someone.

Try kickstarting something new. When my daughter was young, I stopped being timid and alerted my local recreation board to the unmet need I saw for activities for children with disabilities. Our calendar at home was full of activities for all our kids, except one. The recreation board had no idea. How could they? It would take a parent of a child with special needs to open their eyes and hearts to a gap invisible to them. Be that parent.

So began Adapted Sports for Kids, a program I started in my community more than thirty years ago, offering year-round activities for all ages at our local rec center. Embraced by the community and going strong today, the program is a source of fun and friendships for kids with disabilities and their families.

Seeing the talents of many of the kids at the rec center triggered our interest in Special Olympics competition, a step beyond recreation. A group of parents led by my husband, Rick, organized a local chapter and recruited lots of volunteer coaches. Today, our local kids with disabilities are swimmers, cyclists, sprinters, golfers, bowlers, basketball players, and powerlifters. They practice hard and haul in the medals—gold, silver, and bronze—taking pride in their accomplishments and in each other.

Several years ago, Special Olympics asked our group to pilot a new program, called Young Athletes, for little ones aged 2 to 7. In no time, we rallied fresh volunteers—cool college grads inspired by their own experiences having classmates with disabilities. Soon local middle-school, high-school, and college teams volunteered to lead sessions, teaching tots to kick, throw, run, jump, hop, cheer, and have fun.

This program offers a side benefit for parents, too, as they tap into a natural support group on the bleachers while watching their children play together.

In our family, Young Athletes proved to be a matchmaker for Noni's sister, Jacy, who met her future husband, Johnny, while volunteering. They both share an affection for individuals with disabilities.

These three neighborhood programs are collectively known as All-In, and the cycle has come full circle today—as many of the earliest participants are now adults and have become volunteers themselves, experiencing how good it feels to reverse roles and be able to help others.

Brendan, Billy, Sarah, Caitlyn, Tim, Kyle, Jason, Ryan, and Ryan have grown up to be in charge, mentor, and make a difference as they coach little ones with disabilities who need their help and look up to them. Good feelings abound in this gymnasium.

In the 1960s, upon learning kids with intellectual disabilities had nowhere to go for summer camp, Eunice Kennedy Shriver said, "Enough," and started Camp Shriver on her farm in Maryland.

She asked special schools and clinics in her area to provide names of children who might be interested. Then she recruited twenty-six high-school and college students to be counselors and work almost one-on-one with thirty-four children.

A distinct feature of the camp was Shriver's insistence on interaction between children with special needs and typical children. What foresight! The children swam, kicked soccer balls, shot baskets, and rode horses under the summer sun with their counselors. It was an instant success and the origin of the global Special Olympics movement we know today, all led by the force of one woman.

On a much smaller scale, maybe you could start something fun in your neighborhood for your child? Yes, parents of kids with special needs have their hands full and get tired, but we also draw energy from connecting and seeing our kids flourish. These community activities can actually keep us going too.

Organize playtime, summer picnics, or afternoons at the splash park with a group of parents and kids. March in your home-days parade. Approach your local rec center, theater, science center, swim team, or zoo with ideas for including individuals with special needs in their programming. Enlist others' help.

You will enrich your child's life and plenty of others. It's not that hard.

Just do it. For fun.

Could your team use an extra right fielder?

Playing summer baseball was a ritual for all the kids in our house, and Noni was no exception. Then again, yes, she was.

She enjoyed playing baseball with her special-needs friends, she absolutely did. But I hoped at age ten she could participate on a typical girls' baseball team as well, because I thought she'd love the experience in a whole new way.

My best shot at making this happen was to piggyback on her tomboy little sister, a slugger at the plate. Could I propose them as a package deal, a twofer, a BOGO? Dare I ask the coach? How could we make it work and be a win-win for everybody?

The answer came out of right field when the coach was open to having her play extra right field on her sister's team, and the league agreed.

Batting was tricky, but we worked that out too. She would lead off in the first and fourth innings, swing the bat with coach's hand-over-hand help, hit the ball, run to first base, then step off the bag to become assistant first-base coach. And when she did, the crowd on both sides of the field cheered her on.

All season long, she never touched a ball in the field, but she talked it up plenty by mimicking her teammates:

- "Two down, one to go."
- "Play's at second."
- "Nice catch."

As if she knew the game!

She loved sporting a bright team T-shirt, going for ice cream with all the girls after games, and taking home a trophy when they came in first place. We couldn't ask for more.

But there was more. The shocker came at the end of the season when she won the award for highest batting average. You've got to be kidding, I thought. She did make contact but rarely hit the ball past pitcher's mound.

"She batted 1.000," the coach said, smiling. "She made it to first base every time she was up."

It hadn't occurred to me until then but, come to think of it, she *was* always safe at first. Funny thing, no player on any of the opposing teams could ever manage to get her out. Girls muffed the ball, overthrew it, or couldn't outrun her. Each opponent—on her own with no coaching—made sure this player with special needs felt the thrill of getting to first base.

They showed everyone what it means, in sports and in life, to play with heart.

Let's talk about my daughter's period

Every student who receives special education services has an individual education plan, and every parent can attest that the yearly process of crafting it with school officials can be a struggle.

In one of our most memorable meetings, the subject of our daughter's menstrual period dominated the conversation. Noni was making a big transition from middle school to high school. We weren't nervous, but the high school sure was.

My husband and I gathered with a team of educators, therapists, counselors, and administrators to discuss our daughter's goals for the coming year and the school's commitment to providing services to reach them.

I've learned over the years to wear big-girl panties to this party because no parent escapes the occasional IEP meeting from hell. This one went straight down the toilet with the unveiling of their first proposed goal: Manage all personal hygiene needs independently, without assists. Code words for dealing with her period.

Do we spot a stretch goal designed more for the benefit of staff than student?

"Believe me, no one wants to see her reach this goal more than this guy," I said, empathetically, putting my arm around my husband. "He already knows more about wings than he ever wanted to."

Discomfort filled the air. "Yes, let's talk about her period." I smiled, as imaginary thought bubbles around the table shrieked, "Let's not!"

I expressed concern that a goal involving so many motor skills was unrealistic. Our daughter's neurological deficits impede her ability to plan, execute, remember, and transfer motor skills without literally thousands of repetitions.

For example, it took her three years of practice to learn to jump in a pool, five years to learn to throw a ball, and fifteen years of beginner lessons to learn to swim!

Seemingly simple stuff is anything but simple for her. When it takes years and years for a kid to learn a small skill, you carefully choose the skills that matter most.

To get the conversation flowing, I jumped in with a multitude of motor-related questions about the school bathrooms:

- How do the stall doors lock and unlock?
- How do the toilet paper dispensers work?
- How do the toilets flush?
- Where are the receptacles for personal hygiene products and how do they open?
- How do the faucets turn on and off?
- How does the soap dispense?
- What about hand drying?

Blank stares. No one here had carefully weighed or appreciated the complexity of being independent in a public bathroom.

We hadn't even gotten to questions about sanitary napkins! How would she get the darn thing out of the packaging and correctly place the adhesive side down? Ouch!

Who can blame them for not having the answers? Who thinks about stuff like this? I wish I didn't have to.

Have you ever paid attention to how many different kinds of door locks, toilet-paper holders, soap dispensers, faucets, hand towels, dryers, and waste receptacles are in every public bathroom? We all perform a jumble of motor skills just to get in and out.

No, our daughter would not be spending high school in the lavatory! Strike that goal. She needs assistance. Period.

Learning can be a chore

I'm a mother of three once-and-done kids and one over-and-over-again kid.

Three read, listen, watch, do, practice, and learn. Done. That was fun and easy. One tries for days, weeks, months, years, or forever. We do it again and again because that's how she learns. "I'm still working on it," she says and smiles.

When the time came for Noni to enter high school, I questioned the resources for students with disabilities to learn and practice life skills:

- How can you learn to cook in the kitchen without a kitchen?
- How can you learn to wash and dry clothes without a washer and dryer?
- How can you learn to make a bed without a bed?

Logical questions, I thought. But school folks thought I was nuts, exchanging wacky looks around the table during our annual goal-setting meeting.

Learning life skills—such as healthy habits, household basics, money matters, and personal safety—is essential and can be more important than academics for students with developmental disabilities.

These students often have difficulty transferring book learning to real life. Many cannot acquire or master basic skills by reading, listening, or watching. They need hands-on practice and lots of repetition. Mind-numbing repetition. It's how they learn.

Noni's been working on basic life skills basically her whole life, making extraordinary progress at the pace of a snail.

To accommodate the need for repetitive hands-on practice of life skills—and after a full-out, voices-raised, promise-of-due-process battle with us—school administrators agreed to build a daily living center. Thank you.

The prospect of a twin bed in the high school, however, understandably gave them pause. Ultimately, they reasoned there's no substitute for hands-on learning.

Helpful innovations can make life easier for kids like Noni who have trouble with motor skills. For example, an EyeVac dustpan automatically sucks up dirt and crumbs "swiffered" into it. A lightweight cordless vacuum makes fluffing the carpet an easy chore. With Beddy's bed sets, the task of making the bed is as simple as zipping.

With a bed at home and at school, Noni got lots of practice. Before then, she made a lousy bed, likely influenced by the lazy example of her siblings. But at school, learning to make a bed became fun and a source of pride when she sort of mastered it, plus or minus a few wrinkles.

She's been doing it at home every morning ever since, with a smile and an exclamation, "I did it!"

Better than her siblings.

Put on the boxing gloves

I was stoked to check out the new daily living center set to open on the first day of Noni's sophomore year. We'd been planning it with school officials for a year, with construction to take place over the summer.

As inclusion students advanced to high school, it became apparent the building lacked space for this kind of hands-on learning. To solve the problem, we designed a super-sized classroom complete with a café, kitchen, laundry room, and living and dining areas, outfitted with furniture and appliances.

Here, students would learn to launder practice jerseys, prepare and serve food, set the table, clean up, vacuum, make a bed, and more. All high schoolers were welcome in the café during free time, as their friends with special needs served them and made some small change.

I couldn't wait to have a first look, but I wasn't prepared for what I saw.

Nothing.

The construction never got started. Evidently, sometime over the summer, administrators determined they didn't have enough money in the budget to build and furnish the daily living center they'd promised.

I felt blindsided. It was more than a shame. It was a blatant violation of state requirements for public schools to meet basic educational needs of students with disabilities. Time to call an emergency meeting for the very next morning.

Special education teachers, counselors, therapists, and administrators filled the room.

"Where's the principal?" I asked.

"It's the second day of school, and he's busy," came the reply.

"No problem." I glanced at my husband. "We can wait."

During the twenty minutes the principal took to get there, the room was uncomfortably silent as we sat still.

He arrived. He was sorry to disappoint us. The district simply didn't have the money for the project, he said.

Now it was my turn to unleash:

- "I went to the first football game of the season Friday night and saw a team of football players fully outfitted with jerseys and safety gear; a squad of cheerleaders shaking pom-poms; and a marching band decked out with uniforms, instruments, flags and batons, all arriving to the stadium by school bus. Last I checked, these are extracurricular activities."

- "I'm the last person who wants to see sports go away. My other three kids are all student athletes. But, I'm not willing to fund sports at the expense of basic education for students with special needs."

- "Don't tell me the cost of sports comes out of another budget. Money is fungible."

- "What is the budget for this project? What do you mean you don't know? That admission signals you were never serious."

- "Do you realize abiding by state law is not an option, it's a mandate? Right now, you are breaking the law. When are you planning to follow it? I *will* exercise my right to due process to advocate not only for my daughter but for all students with special needs in this school whose individual education plans you cannot meet because there's no place for them to learn independent living skills. Don't make me do it."

- "When all of you in this room found out the daily living center was on the chopping block, did any of you advocate for your students or for following the law? I guess not."

- "Did someone just suggest finding furniture at Goodwill to outfit the center? Do you purchase from Goodwill for the regular education students? No? Then why would you think I would sit still watching my other kids get brand new while this one gets used?"

- "I'm going to give you a chance to rethink the daily living center. You're welcome."

I've always told school officials and teachers my job is laser focused on crusading for Noni. I believe it's my duty and the reason God gave her to me.

Their jobs, I appreciate, are more complex. They have other students and responsibilities, including budgets, in their purview.

"If we ever disagree," I say, "it's not personal. I'm just doing my job. We can still be friends."

Good news came that very afternoon. After scrambling to figure out logistics, school officials resurrected the daily living center project, complete with a budget, timeline, and an anticipated grand opening three months later. It took a tense meeting full of differing views and high emotions, but we came together to get it done. The center turned out fabulous.

And we're still friends.

"OPTIMISMS" TO LIVE BY

DO YOU care if something has never been done before? No, not when you're a parent of a child with special needs. You get better at pushing and insisting, "Let's give this idea a try!" You become strong enough to not take no for an answer. Because you will do whatever it takes to create opportunities for your child, even if it means doing it yourself.

Say Hello to Giggles and Goofiness

Until we find cures, learning to live your best life in the present is the way forward.
DR. KONARK MUKHERJEE, researcher investigating CASK gene disorder

IN HIS laboratory at the University of Alabama at Birmingham in the Department of Genetics at the Heersink School of Medicine, Dr. Konark Mukherjee knows his work is a long crusade.

I meet parents of children with neurodevelopmental conditions desperate for a cure. It's good for parents and researchers alike to have hope. We must. But while we work toward a cure, life goes on. The smartest approaches we can offer these children now are intensive therapies, early education, acceptance in schools and communities, welcoming workplaces, no limits, unconditional love, and, don't forget, large doses of fun and laughter, all of which can lead to a full life.

My daughter has lived forty years with multiple disabilities and no cure, but she has had plenty of opportunities to live a wonderful life. Her extended family, friends, inclusive education, part-time job, sports, and activities all add up to bring her fulfillment and joy.

As her mother, I've gained expertise in the lived life, making the most of everything we could offer her, short of a cure. It's the only treatment we have. And it works.

Crack me up, buttercup!

Life with a child with disabilities can be comical, and it's okay to laugh!

Young Graham, a preschooler with CASK gene disorder, was a handful the day his teacher sent this message home to his mom, Allie: "Your son is being a CASKhole today." Mom burst out laughing and replied, "Every day!"

She shared the teacher's note with other moms of kids with CASK, including me, who chimed in, "Mine too! Mine too!"

When preteen Alana, affectionately known as LaLa, sat down to breakfast, she saw an egg-white omelet staring back at her. Not just any omelet, but one proudly whipped up by her dad, Scott, a self-described world-series-champion omelet maker. LaLa is nonverbal and reached for her communication device. She quickly pressed a few buttons on her talker to say, "I want french toast."

"Not today," said Dad.

"I want french toast," she repeated, scowling.

Say Hello to Giggles and Goofiness   111

Life with a child with disabilities can be comical, and it's okay to laugh!

"Well today, sweetie," he explained, "we're having eggs."

Her fingers pounded madly on her talker to express precisely what she was thinking: "Ain't that some bullshit!"

In the next room, her mother howled. Scott tried but quickly failed to keep his composure. He was tickled because his daughter with limited ability to communicate used the indelicate slang in the proper manner to insult her daddy!

Our family roars at recollections of infamous "Noni Baloney" moments. Like the time we walked into Uncle Melvin's wake to greet the family. In this solemn space for all to hear, Noni blurted, "Megan, you've got a booger on your nose!"

Cousin Megan, mortified, explained in a hushed tone that it was a nose ring.

Noni would have none of it.

Fully confident she knows a booger when she sees one, she adamantly upped the volume of her voice. "No, no, no, you've got a booger on your nose, right there," she said, poking Megan's nose with her index finger.

A contingent of cousins lost it, and contagious laughter filled the funeral parlor. Megan will never live it down.

Uncle Melvin would be howling.

In high school, during Monday morning conversations about "What I Did Over the Weekend," Noni let her classmates know, "I started my period."

After a quick reminder about not sharing private information, her teacher redirected her by asking what else happened. "My sister started hers too."

The girl is a free spirit. So proud of herself after successfully undressing independently before bath time, she appeared in her brother's bedroom, beaming and naked, exclaiming, "Look at me! I did it all by myself!" She's quite comfortable in her own skin.

Her sibs love to tell the story of her bikini-top malfunction on a water slide when she was a teenager. Her total cluelessness at the scene of the mishap still reduces them to fits of laughter.

Her favorite phrase on exiting the bathroom is, "I feel better now." She can't help asking guests who use our bathroom, "Do you feel better now?"

When it comes to spreading mirth, she's unwittingly got the gift.

Lizards, turtles, and frogs, oh my!

Ours is a petless family, but not for lack of trying.

I always thought having a pet would be good for our kids, Noni especially. Simba the cat was our first attempt, but a year later when allergy-prone Jacy developed asthma, Simba moved to our cousin's house for the next twenty-two years. At least we saw him on holidays!

Since all critters with fur were out of the question for us, we had to get creative. On a vacation in Florida, the kids captured a tiny yard lizard and kept it alive by feeding it bugs and water. "Please, please, please," they begged, "can we take Lizzy home with us?" I was pretty sure on our twenty-hour drive to Ohio, Lizzy wouldn't make it to Georgia, so I said yes.

Lizzy lived her full two-year lifespan in Ohio in the comfort of her tricked-out glass habitat, with a steady diet of freeze-dried flies and water, treated occasionally to a live ant or spider. The kids loved showing her off, especially each time she outgrew and shed her skin.

Our oldest came home from college with a giant stocked fish tank, something he knew I wouldn't want, so he thoughtfully bought Noni her very own turtle the size of a quarter to add to the tank, making it impossible for me to say no. We were stuck with a fish tank in the foyer.

Noni named her new turtle Bee Bop and waved to him every day on her way in and out the front door. Soon he was the size of a hockey puck, the largest creature in the aquarium.

When Bee Bop appeared lethargic one day, I became worried because of Noni's presumed attachment to him. I took him an hour's drive to a turtle vet, where they pronounced him malnourished. Who knew turtles could not live on fish food alone? They pumped him with nutrients, and $100 later we were on our way home.

"You spent how much?!" my husband gasped.

I set newly invigorated Bee Bop back on his lily pad, where he performed a swan dive to the bottom of the tank and expired.

Ever so gently, we explained to Noni that Bee Bop went to turtle heaven. Matter-of-factly, she snapped, "That's it. He's gone." For closure, we buried Bee Bop under a rock in our yard, with the kids irreverently groaning, "This is ridiculous, Mom. Can we go now?"

Just when I thought we were done trying out pets, those same kids gave Noni two dwarf frogs in a Frog-O-Sphere for Christmas. We named them Sunday and Thursday because those were the days we fed them their pellets. I wasn't sad when they died several years later, until those blasted kids went out and bought Noni two more! We named these Monday and Friday. They're gone now too.

After trial and error, alas, we've hit on the perfect pet for Noni! Snickerdoodle is her beloved weighted stuffed bulldog with sensory powers who sits on her lap, sleeps with her at night, and goes on vacations with us. Getting the plushy through TSA at the airport can be tricky, but he's low maintenance otherwise.

With time, he has a tendency to develop rips and tatters and his stuffing falls out. We treat him to a spa day and when he comes home, he looks and smells brand new! (Wink wink.)

He's a keeper!

Finding Mr. Nice Guy

A baseball buff, Matt knows all there is to know about major leaguers, and he can hardly contain himself on what turns out to be a perfect night for baseball in Cleveland.

From his seat in the ballpark, he transforms into a color commentator, spouting batting averages, earned-run averages, and lifetime stats for every player at the plate. His mom, Kris, cringes on the edge of her seat as innings go by, worrying the fans around them are becoming annoyed with her son's unrelenting exuberance.

Until Matt commits an error. He's wrong about which team the batter at the plate once played for. The fan in front of him turns around to say, "Gotcha," correcting and high-fiving him at the same time.

Matt's face suddenly sports the biggest, broadest grin. He shakes his fists in front of his eyes, because that's what Matt does when he's super happy, an endearing gesture his whole family imitates when they're happy too.

Thank you, Mr. Nice Guy. You shared your love of the game with a young boy with intellectual disabilities and helped make the night enjoyable for everyone. Mom could rest easy, and Matt could be his joyful, baseball-loving self. Bet you felt pretty good too.

Families out with their children with special needs are buoyed by small gestures of kindness.

Families out and about with their children with special needs are buoyed by seemingly small gestures of kindness:

- A smile. It conveys you're okay walking patiently behind us as we escort our slowpoke down the bleachers safely.

- Applause. It's uplifting when you admire her effort in the school music show. Never mind her rocking to the beat during the otherwise motionless choir performance and missing every beat in the song and dance number.

- A wave. It means a lot from the perspective of a person in a wheelchair and to the parent behind the wheels.

- A question. You acknowledge him and give him a chance to express himself when you ask, "When is your birthday?" or "What kind of dressing do you want on your salad?"

- Teasing. Who doesn't enjoy joking around! Go ahead and greet her at the hair salon with, "Hey, Toots, looks like you need some beautifying!"
- A compliment. "Good call, Mr. Baseball Stats" praises his skill.

And sends Matt's fists shaking wildly in front of his eyes.

When in Rome

Noni is always up for an adventure, perhaps because she has no idea what to expect. We simply tell her how much fun we're going to have, and she believes us.

Like jumping waves in the ocean. It's a blast until she gets tossed by a big wave and face plants in the sand. Way to go, we acclaim. Score that a 10! Gimme a high five!

Disoriented and not sure what just happened, she's definitely having second thoughts. This little mishap calls for a distraction. Hey, who wants to look for seashells?

We knew taking Noni and sister Jacy on a vacation abroad would be challenging, but we were up for it. We're going to Italy! That's really all she needed to know. We left out the part about hours of walking, climbing, and sleeping scrunched up on airplanes.

We scouted a few hiking trails when we arrived to ensure she'd be safe. When her sister declared, "She'll kill herself on that one," we crossed it off our list.

We sped through several major attractions. When Noni was feeling cultural overload, "enough statues" and "no more churches" signaled time to move on, folks. She has a flair for putting into words what others are silently thinking.

When she looked up at more steps than she wanted to climb (again), she wouldn't budge, until coaxing, clapping, and cheering her on—Who's gonna be the winner?—propelled her to the top. We do whatever it takes.

Just when it seemed we were breezing through Italy along the shores of Cinque Terre and the cobblestone streets of Rome, we came flush with a surprising obstacle that stopped us in our tracks. After enjoying a fancy Italian dinner with wine (yes, Noni would like a glass to clink. Cheers, everybody!), a trip to the ladies' room found us gaping into a deep, dark hole in the ground, also known as a squat toilet.

Noni cannot squat.

Jacy and I realized the urgency of figuring out a solution before Noni peed her pants. We formed a plan and sprang into action.

First, both of us demonstrated for her how it's done. When it was Noni's turn, Jacy secured her under the armpits, and I grabbed her under the knees. We lowered her into a squatting position on this unconventional throne and coaxed her to let it go, knowing full well she would have no ability to aim. That job would fall to us too.

Cradled in our arms and getting heavier by the minute, Noni burst out laughing! And so did we, trying with all our might not to drop this stinker in the hole!

Bathroom tales are lore in families managing special needs, as we find improbable ways to navigate hindrances. Dads take daughters into the men's room when moms aren't there. Likewise, with moms and sons. Everyone in the family, including brothers and sisters, learn to help wipe when pressed into service.

It's not always pretty, but sometimes it can be pretty funny.

How to land on the Midnight List

In our house, you don't want to wind up on Noni's famous Midnight List. It means you've done something to set her off, and now you're in big trouble. We've all been there.

When it happens, Noni runs to the kitchen counter, clutches a marker with a death grip in the palm of her hand, scribbles ferociously on a tablet of paper, then shouts, "That's it! Read it! Right here! You're on the Midnight List."

What her siblings find so funny is that her scribbles are indecipherable blobs, but she repeatedly insists we read the note. Ask her what her note says, she'll bark, "Read it! The whole note."

When my girls were teenagers, younger sister Jacy, not inclined to cut Noni a little slack, was a frequent flyer on the Midnight List. The two shared a bedroom and on a rare morning when Jacy could sleep in, she'd yell at Noni to "Be quiet! Get out!" That'll get you on the Midnight List.

So will helping yourself to your sister's clothes. Jacy made the mistake of wearing one of Noni's T-shirts, knowing full well her callous disregard would cause her sister to freak out. When it happened, unremorseful Jacy escalated the bickering:

Noni: "Take it off, or you're going on the Midnight List!"

Jacy: "Go ahead. Put me on the Midnight List. I don't care!"

Noni: "That's it. You're going to bed at midnight!"

Jacy: "That's fine with me! Do you realize going to bed at midnight is not a punishment? Actually, it would be a treat!"

Noni: "That's it. You're on it."

Jacy: "Don't you get it? The Midnight List is stupid and makes no sense."

Noni: "You're on the Midnight List—again!"

Jacy: "You made up the whole silly thing, and it's totally illogical."

Illogical? I jumped into the fray and snapped at Jacy, "Look who you, Miss Smarty Pants, are debating logic with!"

Expressing feelings of frustration can be difficult for those with intellectual disabilities. Noni's Midnight List is a healthy, harmless way for her to vent. It allows her to stick up for herself and take charge.

The Midnight List lives on in our home on the kitchen counter long after her siblings have moved away. Now, it's Mom and Dad's turn to land on the list for all kinds of infractions:

- "No bath tonight. I took a bath yesterday." (No, she didn't.)

- "You got sunscreen in my eyes. It burns. No more."

- "No ponytail. I like my hair down."

- "It's *my* job to get the mail. Put it back."
- "These shoes hurt my feet."
- "I don't like ham."
- "Ouch. You brushed my teeth too hard."

If this is the extent of your complaints about your parents, I'd say you've got it pretty good, sister.

"OPTIMISMS" TO LIVE BY

TEASE YOUR kids. Blow raspberries on their bellies. Laugh out loud. When you do, you're releasing endorphins, and you need all the endorphins you can get when you're juggling lifelong disabilities. Bring a healthy balance to your life by making fun and good times a priority—for them and you.

Thank You to the Trailblazers

*In the early 1900s, words like "idiot," "imbecile,"
and "moron" were medical terms used to classify
individuals with a wide range of differences.*
ANDREW SOLOMON, award-winning American author,
Far from the Tree

ONE OF the most phenomenal books I've ever read, Andrew Solomon's *Far from the Tree*, moves us beyond the world's despicable history of eugenics to stories of triumph today driven largely by parents helping their children become their best selves.

Of an earlier era, Solomon writes:

In a 1927 Supreme Court decision upholding forced sterilization, Justice Oliver Wendell Holmes wrote, "It is better for all the world if... society can prevent those who are manifestly unfit from continuing their kind... Three generations of imbeciles are enough."

In 1968, the ethicist Joseph Fletcher wrote in The Atlantic journal, *that esteemed journal of liberal thought, that there was "no reason to feel guilty about putting a Down syndrome baby away... It is sad, yes. Dreadful. But it carries no guilt. True guilt arises from an offense against a person, and a Down's is not a person."*

Today, no one would publish an article in the mainstream media that championed dehumanizing a group of disabled people as Joseph Fletcher did. What was once par for the course has become unthinkable.

Thank God.

Solomon has brilliantly researched and written on the intensity of life with a severely challenging child. He tells of families coping with Down syndrome, autism, schizophrenia, deafness, dwarfism, multiple severe disabilities, and more. He concludes upliftingly:

These parents have, by and large, chosen to love their children and... value their own lives, even though they carry what most of the world considers an intolerable burden. Most of the families... have ended up grateful for the experiences they would have done anything to avoid.

Who's noneducable?

When Kevin was born in 1965, nurses covered his face with a light blanket in the hospital nursery during visiting hours, the practice at the time for newborns with Down syndrome. His mother, Rose, threw a fit, demanding they unveil him for all the world to see the cherub face of her "child of God."

Not so long ago, not much education of kids with special needs was going on in schools.

This moment would be the first of many times Rose would stand up and shout out for her son.

As a youngster, Kevin was automatically labeled "noneducable," another sign of the times. In colleges in the 1970s, special-education majors could choose from two tracks: EMR or NMR, short for educable mentally retarded and noneducable mentally retarded, words we cringe at hearing today.

Who's noneducable? Who gets to play God and make such a ruinous decision?

Thank goodness we now realize there's no such thing.

Degrees of intellectual disability vary greatly, from mild to moderate to severe to profound. All those with intellectual disability generally develop slower, but where is the proof that they cannot learn? Nowhere. They do learn, but it takes them longer, sometimes a lot longer.

Not so long ago, not much education of kids with special needs was going on in schools, except for the few who could reach the high bar to be labeled "slow learners." The rest typically went to developmental centers or stayed home with no schooling at all.

The eleventh in a family with twelve children, Kevin was the only one who couldn't go to school. Had he been born today, he would have had access to education, which now enables students with disabilities to lead more productive lives.

Over his lifetime of more than thirty years, Kevin flourished in the bosom and chaos of his large clan. He was every sibling's favorite, a great tagalong who benefited from the experience of being included in all aspects of family life.

Raucous family dinner conversations and game-night rivalries gave rise to natural opportunities for him to learn. He became a formidable competitor in Bingo, Monopoly, and Clue, his favorite board game.

He could swim and play basketball, complex skills plenty of people can't perform. What's more, he knew everything there was to know about big-time wrestling.

Kevin had no trouble making friends, as his siblings' friends routinely parading through the house became his friends, too, including a few pretty girls he wanted to marry. Count social skills and affection among his strengths.

He could never understand why some kids laughed at him. It pained him and made him cry. One summer, though, he taught a few taunters a lesson at the pool when they discovered their beach towels at the bottom of the deep end, thanks to Kevin.

The pet names he gave his brothers and sisters—NayNay, RoRo, Assa, Ahi, BooBoo, At, EeeNee, Di, LaLa—live on at family get-togethers, a tender reminder of Kevin. "We always thought he couldn't pronounce our first names," said sister NayNay, "but one day he shocked me when he called me Sharon. That smart cookie had us all fooled for years."

Kevin defied his label, dispelling the general belief that people with Down syndrome could not learn. Even more remarkable, Kevin the learner proved to be an incomparable teacher. He showed those lucky enough to be in his circle how to love, love, love everyone.

An ancient Chinese proverb posits, "Tell me and I forget. Teach me and I remember. Involve me and I will learn."

Centuries later, we're slowly catching on.

"It could've been me."

Fraternal twins Scott and Steve are a rare pair. Born in 1970, Scott has Down syndrome and thirteen-minutes-younger Steve does not. The phenomenon is so rare, it took fifty years for Steve to meet a similar set of twins.

"People would stare," Steve recollects of growing up in a less-than-enlightened era. "I was very conscious we were different, and I hated that kids sometimes were mean to my brother."

The two became fast friends with another pair of brothers in their neighborhood who were also different, one white and one black. The improbable foursome bonded and stood up for each other when acceptance was hard to find.

Without a doubt, times have changed for the better for Scott. In the span of fifty years, people have become kinder, more accepting, and more apt to embrace him.

In fact, today he's seen as something of a celebrity among the locals. He's the prince of his favorite salon, holding court during haircuts and manicures and occasionally blowing kisses when a pretty blonde catches his eye. This gentle jester keeps 'em smiling.

Young people today are often shocked by society's history of cruelty to individuals with Down syndrome and other disabling conditions. But getting to know those with disabilities—really know them—as classmates and friends has made them open and accepting.

Tenderhearted Steve is his brother's keeper and best buddy, and purehearted Scott delights in spending lots of time hanging out together. Their differences eradicate any sibling rivalry and illuminate the love that binds them.

"Taking on parental-like caring for my brother is simply the right thing to do. Do I resent the responsibility? Never. I wouldn't have it any other way," Steve explains. "It could have been me, and I know for certain he would have stepped up."

The two live near each other—Scott in a nice group home with a room of his own, and Steve in a home he shares with his partner, Andy, Scott's biggest fan. Steve has fashioned a life for his twin full of Scott's favorite things:

- Bowling. A can't-miss date at the alleys.

- Big-time wrestling. "I've never met a Down's man who doesn't love professional wrestling," Steve chuckles.

- Holiday trips together. The Big Apple and the Capitol, here they come! Upon arrival at the hotel, Scott shakes hands with everyone and walks away from the front desk giddy with free swag.

- Birthday bash every June 16. Nothing says "happy birthday" like matching polo shirts and pizza. Steve made the mistake of ordering fancy food one year and will never do that again.

- Weekends and Sunday dinners at Steve's place. Where's Scott? Indulging in the home theater, of course.

Scott and Steve. Steve and Scott. Theirs is a brotherly love story of a modern family living happily among the openhearted.

What I learned from Aunt Jo

My Aunt Josephine raised a son with profound intellectual disabilities and cerebral palsy for six decades. Who knew growing up with Cousin Tommy would be great preparation years later for me to raise my own daughter with disabilities?

Aunt Jo was a pioneer in her day. When doctors advised her to put Tommy in an institution in the early 1950s, she wouldn't hear of it and took him home instead. When they told her he would never learn to walk, she tried anyway, and he did.

Aunt Jo brought Tommy to every family gathering always dressed to the nines. She was proud of him. We all loved him.

Tommy had an eye for pretty girls and a talent for flirting. His best girl was his mom. He coined the phrase "Mudder o' mine," a term of endearment for his mother, which has been passed down to all the mothers in our family today. My siblings and I smile and think of Tommy every time we call our mom by this sweet moniker.

Hardship didn't consume Aunt Jo, because she had a knack for finding humor in her life. At his birthday bash when he turned 50, I complimented him on his full head of black hair. "How come you don't have any gray hair like the rest of us?" I teased.

Aunt Jo quipped, "You wouldn't have any gray hair either if somebody wiped your butt every day!"

Years ago on Mother's Day, Aunt Jo and I were in church, where all mothers were saluted. A predictable few were singled out and presented with a red rose: The oldest mother, the newest mother, the mother with the most children.

How about the mother who cares for her child with disabilities every day for a lifetime? Aunt Jo buried her beloved Tommy, who died at 60. Many years later, as her time drew near at the age of 96, she was free of worry because Tommy preceded her and she could die in peace. "You understand," she confided. I do.

Every Mother's Day is for Aunt Jo, and for all aging mothers of children with disabilities who show moms like me how to raise a child, forever.

When our children go before us

I sighed to see Cheryl's name and her sweet, smiling face in the obituaries. She was 57, often out and about in the community, with her mother always nearby. Her mother is sure to miss her terribly yet also find peace in living to see her daughter loved and well cared for her entire life.

The community of families living with special needs has ample experience with death. In our circle, losing classmates with disabilities began when our daughter was in preschool. We lost Becky to seizures and tiny Valerie when she didn't wake up one morning. Then Michael, Brian, Tyne, Sandy, Mikey, and Gregory as time went on.

I imagine God welcoming each of these angels into heaven with outstretched arms and praise, "Well done, my child.

"Yours was a difficult life indeed, and at times you could make life difficult for others too. It was your calling, for you showed them they could conquer difficult, and you made them better for it.

"You are to be commended for the blessings you generously bestowed on others." Indeed, a litany of them:

- Fortitude to the minister. You shout out during his homily. He prays you will stop but, no, you push him to practice what he preaches.

- Friendship to the newlyweds. When they move in next door, you welcome them to the neighborhood. They invite you to stop by anytime, not guessing you will pop over. Every. Single. Day.

- Enlightenment to the doctor. When she asks for your signature, you put your handwriting skills on display, scribbling the form top to bottom, showing her what dyspraxia looks like.

- Harmony to your friends. When you vehemently insist a cow is a horse, they try earnestly to correct you until they learn to let it go. Being right is sometimes overrated.

- Gentleness to the airport security officer. He randomly selects you for screening, commanding you not to touch his drug-sniffing dog until he realizes not petting Fido is not an option for you.

- Perseverance to your teachers. You arrive each day with a clean slate because do-over (and over) is your learning style.

- Patience to your parents. Every mom and dad needs more of this attribute, especially yours!

"The people in your life will need these virtues," God will say, "to get where you're going."

Everybody remembers somebody

The whole baby boomer generation missed out on the inclusion movement, coming of age in an era when kids with disabilities were exempt or turned away from the chance for education. But for those who grew up with someone with disabilities in their neighborhood or family, recollections are strong, as many old friends have recounted.

Peter fondly remembers stories his mother, Mary, would tell about growing up as a teenager in the mid-1930s in a working-class neighborhood in Liverpool, England, a town that long ago accepted people who were different and included them as a matter of course. They used the word "soft" as a term of endearment to describe someone who was different mentally or physically.

Soft Ethel, about 30 at the time, lived on Mary's street and "was always beautifully turned out, with a matching skirt and tam." Ethel liked to play jump rope with the younger girls on the street. When she wanted a turn at jumping, you had to indulge her or she'd "belt you into next week."

Soft Bill lived at the bottom of the street and was always in a wheelchair. His mother put him on the corner of the street while she cleaned house. "If we were going down to the shops, we always took Soft Bill with us," Mary recounted. "We pushed his chair there, went into the shops, then pushed him back and left him by his porch. It was a bit of a change for him."

In a blue-collar neighborhood of cookie-cutter bungalows in Ohio, Mary Beth grew up with Valley and Jackie, two girls with disabilities. Valley had Down syndrome and few words in her vocabulary. Jackie was blind. The other kids were boys.

"Jackie was allowed to play at her house or yard only, so I went there and played dolls with her all the time. Her mother knitted outfits for our Tammy dolls, and we both had a full wardrobe to play with.

"I always thought it odd, though, that she wasn't allowed to leave the familiarity of her own space. She didn't come play at my house. You see, I didn't realize Jackie was blind until my mom told me years later."

Valley couldn't play dolls or board games, explained Mary Beth, "but she liked to come over my house for lunch and have a jelly sandwich with me.

She'd spend all day outside, watching us kids play, participating when she could. She loved hiding and being found when we played kick the can. She'd stay out with us until dusk when the streetlights went on. All the parents and kids watched out for her. Times were much different then."

Susan's best friend growing up had a brother, Chris, with infectious joy and Down syndrome. Susan's father would make toys for Chris, like a set of hoops made of plastic tubing with colored water inside, which he never tired of. Homemade sensory toys!

As a teenager, Susan remembers hanging out with him during summer vacation watching reruns of the TV show *That Girl* starring Marlo Thomas. "I loved that show and wanted to be just like her. At the end of the intro she would muss up her hair, and Chris would always muss up his hair too. I'd laugh, which of course encouraged him to do it more. Oh, what he brought to our lives!"

When Noni was little, I approached Carl, the recreation director in our community, imploring him to take the lead in offering activities for kids with special needs in the community. I was armed with a solid rationale, ready to go to bat for these kids. Before I could launch into my spiel, he responded with a single word: "Done."

What I didn't know? Carl grew up with a brother with Down syndrome. He understood perfectly and made it happen.

Years later, as all our children and their many friends have grown up, I've witnessed firsthand the positive influence of Noni in their lives. Jacy's friend Jossie and Trent's friend Chad each went on to marry and have children with special needs.

Jossie recalls:

I saw the way your kids were with her and how she had amazing parents who always advocated for her needs. Everything your family did and does for Noni and the countless hours you must have spent talking with teachers, staff, and therapists, I see it so much more clearly now. I think of your family often as I am raising my own children.

Noni was one of us growing up! She would always tag along and could make us laugh until we cried. She was always so kind to everyone, I remember thinking to myself, "Wow, what if we all lived the way she does."

My hope is to surround my children with other positive and accepting children and families who will make them feel loved. The world may think they have disabilities, but I like to think it's their superpower.

For everyone, knowing someone with disabilities leaves a lasting mark.

Chad agrees. He said:

Growing up across the street from Noni and her siblings had a huge impact on me, though I didn't truly realize the extent until years later. She was always included in everything we did, never a second thought about her playing baseball or other games with us. Being friends with her naturally taught me to accept others. Watching Noni thrive at school, participate in sports, and always receive the support she needed from her family has taught me how to advocate for my own child.

Chad's daughter Claire, a micropreemie born at twenty-two weeks weighing one pound and one ounce and diagnosed with cerebral palsy, is now a thriving 4-year-old who loves to read books, make friends, and play any sport possible. She navigates in her "walking wagon," a.k.a. gait trainer, as she works on walking independently.

"I have relied on every member of Noni's family in one way or another," says Chad, "knowing they understand and could help us with knowledge to better advocate for our daughter with specialists, therapists, and teachers.

We want Claire to be included and have a fulfilling life, and we can't wait to see what the future holds for her."

The good news is today more young people than ever before have opportunities to be profoundly touched by someone with disabilities, thanks to inclusion.

Because for everyone, knowing someone with disabilities leaves a lasting mark.

"OPTIMISMS" TO LIVE BY

WHAT A difference a hundred years makes. We cringe to think about the way things were for individuals with all kinds of disabilities. Parents who pushed boundaries back then collectively paved the way for us to raise our children today in the embrace of our society, with a right to education, employment, and belonging in the community. Now, we must carry the torch.

Suddenly, They're Adults

*The baker hired Simone and everybody saw
that she could do the job.*
"THE HIRING CHAIN" PERFORMED BY STING

"THE HIRING CHAIN," sung by cool dude Sting for World Down Syndrome Day, was written and produced in collaboration with Italian nonprofit Coor-Down, the New York agency Small, Stabbiolo Music, and Indiana Production. Beautiful lyrics like these, reprinted here with permission, have the power to move people:

The baker hired Simone and everybody saw that she could do the job.
  The lawyer went to the baker and saw Simone at work.
  The lawyer hired John because the baker hired Simone, the baker hired Simone.
  The dentist went to the lawyer and saw John at work.
  The dentist hired Sophia because the lawyer hired John because the baker hired Simone, the baker hired Simone.

The farmer went to the dentist and saw Sophia at work.

The farmer hired Kate because the dentist hired Sophia because the lawyer hired John because the baker hired Simone, the baker hired Simone.

The barber went to the farmer and saw Kate at work.

The barber hired Paul because the farmer hired Kate because the dentist hired Sophia because the lawyer hired John because the baker hired Simone, the baker hired Simone.

The baker went to the barber and saw Paul at work.

He didn't have a clue but it was thanks to his first move that...

The barber hired Paul because the farmer hired Kate because the dentist hired Sophia because the lawyer hired John because the baker hired Simone, the baker hired Simone.

I urge you to treat yourself to a listen on YouTube. Guarantee you'll replay it over and over. The more we turn employers on to this song and its aspirational message, the more adults with a mix of capabilities and disabilities will be hired.

Play it forward.

Here's how careers are created

"Marching off the cliff" is how many parents of young adults with special needs describe what's next after high school ends. Our daughter was lucky to have a soft landing, falling into a career of fruits and vegetables.

People are always surprised to learn Noni has a job, this kid of ours who cannot read, distinguish a dime from a quarter, or make a phone call.

Don't be discouraged if your child's need for accommodations is great. Go for great.

Invariably, the next question is, "What does she do?"

Lots of things very well, thank you. She works mornings in the produce department of our neighborhood grocery store, family-owned Heinen's, where coworkers and job coaches have trained her on a variety of tasks that don't require reading or math skills. It's been her happy place for more than eighteen years.

Adults with disabilities can connect with job coaches typically through vocational schools, transition programs, and government agencies. Job coaches help train individuals on the job until they master the tasks required.

Unlike most job coaches, Noni's never fades away, but stays with her on the job, a key accommodation she needs and one well worth fighting for. Permanent job coaches allow kids and adults with disabilities to work when they otherwise might not be able to. For parents unsure whether or not their child will one day work, it's another creative option worth exploring.

Don't be discouraged if your child's need for accommodations is great, like my daughter's. Go for great and get her what she needs to succeed as an adult.

Noni is handy with lettuce, potatoes, broccoli, carrots,

tomatoes, onions, and cucumbers, to name an assortment. She's a big fan of oranges and adept at dropping them into the fresh-squeeze machine. Above all, she loves, loves, loves plucking grapes off stems for meal prepping and has become expert at it.

Performing these basic duties challenges and fulfills her while freeing her coworkers to focus on higher-level work. A win-win.

Sometimes people ask if she's a bagger, the stereotypical job of individuals with disabilities working in grocery stores. Heck no! That responsibility is way above her pay grade. It requires fine-motor skills to open the bag and cognitive awareness not to pack the jar of pickles atop the hotdog buns.

Hats off to those who can do it, like her adept friend Matthew, with congenital toxoplasmosis and developmental disabilities, who's a master bagger and a master charmer as well.

Another friend Greg, with autism, is a masterful shredder. His employer can count on him to shred every document with lips-zipped confidentiality while livening up the office.

More than thirty-five years ago, the inclusion movement sprouted in the classroom, then quickly spread way beyond into scout troops, baseball teams, homecoming courts, college campuses, and now the workplace.

Employees with special needs represent the next wave of diversity entering the workforce. They can enrich the culture of organizations and the empathy of employees in ways no one else can. If you're early in your journey with disability, don't underestimate your child's future.

If you're early in your journey with disability, don't underestimate your child's future.

Hiring them is not that hard.

Just ask Mr. Kelly, a vocational schoolteacher who, year after year, used his ingenuity to create and land jobs for students with disabilities. Having done it a hundred times over, he's worthy of a spot in the National Inventors Hall of Fame.

His winning formula? Focus on one student at a time. Imagine a job tailored to her strengths. Sell the idea and the student to a local employer willing to try.

When standard job descriptions don't perfectly fit individuals with special needs, he looks for a workaround, not an excuse not to hire them. Limitations of his students activate Mr. Kelly's imagination, and his can-do passion opens the minds of employers to think accommodatingly.

Mr. Kelly sets up students to succeed, surrounding them with job coaches and "natural supports," a fancy phrase for caring coworkers. Students start as unpaid interns until graduation, then they become competitively paid employees.

Millennials and Gen Z are among the best natural supports in the workplace, thanks to their inclusion experience in school. They see capability where earlier generations see disability, and they are comfortable living, working, and playing together. To them, it's second nature.

Yet most employers are not tapping into this resource in their organizations. Young people themselves fail to recognize this competency of theirs is something special. Wake up, people!

Enlightened employers are hiring transporters in hospitals and airports, servers in school cafeterias, food-prep assistants in restaurants, gardeners in nurseries, mail clerks in company headquarters, scanners and basic coders in data centers.

A variety of job opportunities, full time and part time, can be created at local cafés, bakeries, fitness centers, farms, museums, gift shops, pet stores, kennels, retail stores, fast-food chains, and many other caring businesses, sometimes just by asking.

Entrepreneurs with developmental disabilities can be responsible dog walkers and pet sitters for family, friends, and neighbors.

Noni is an uber-engaged employee. She sees grocery shoppers all around town and excitedly exchanges a friendly wave or hello. Often, I ask, "Who's that?" or "How do you know that person?"

With a strut, a smile, and a fist bump, she declares proudly, "That's my customer!" to the friend smiling back.

Finding purpose after graduation

What's next?

It's the big worry for parents whose children age out of school and are unlikely to find employment in the conventional labor market.

Fortunately, more and more creative alternatives are blossoming thanks to entrepreneurs touched by special needs. Denise Hazen, in Houston, Texas, is one such mom. She wouldn't accept the doctor's early prediction that her son Nick, diagnosed with autism, would never be a productive member of society.

Instead, she took matters into her own hands to create meaningful employment for him and kids like him. Denise founded Aspire Accessories (aspireaccessories.com), a thriving nonprofit employing and training dozens of individuals with neurological differences.

"We provide a solution to what is known as the 'services cliff' for this population of individuals once they age out of supported school-based environments," she explains on her website.

Artisans here earn competitive wages while learning job skills in a supportive environment. They make and sell online a wide range of handmade goods like embroidered napkins and ball caps, leather bracelets and lariat necklaces, acrylic earrings and serving trays, candles and coasters, and lots more. Employees also build business skills from inventory to sales.

For some, Aspire Accessories is a landing pad for supportive, long-term employment and skill-building. For others, it's a launchpad to learn new skills in preparation for future employment or higher education.

For Denise, it's building a community of artisans and showcasing their talents.

In San Diego, California, Rita Saliba Nasrallah, also worried about the future for Michael, her teenage son with autism. She saw many individuals on the autism spectrum living in group homes, not contributing to their communities. Those who found jobs often eventually lost or left them.

The disconnect she observed for individuals whose disabilities are significant and lifelong was lack of continuing support in the workplace, the very key to their success in school. "Just as we tailored school programs to facilitate learning for children with autism, why not create small businesses tailored for them when they age out of the school system? Why not give them a chance to continue to actively participate in their communities?" Good question.

Believing in the ability of individuals with autism and developmental disabilities to reach their potential with the right support, Rita started Blissful Seeds (blissfulseeds.org) in her garage. Today, her growing nonprofit enterprise operates out of a retail storefront, selling products handmade by adults with special needs at the gift shop and online.

These makers feel proud to see their novelty soaps and bath bombs, healing bead bracelets, potted houseplants, and one-of-a-kind paintings fly off the shelves.

Not all young adults with developmental disabilities are headed to employment, yet they, too, are seeking a meaningful life when they complete school. What are their options?

In Cleveland, Ohio, Bess Vrettos began Christine's Hope (inclusionworksoh.org), a robust day program, in memory of her sister with special needs. To say it's not your typical day program is an understatement. "It's a dream and a labor of love for me," she says, "and for all our volunteers too."

Bess is a visionary, and Christine's Hope is her vision. Her redefined model stands out with its strategy to engage its citizens, as participants are called, with the community.

Sweetie Pies Bakery, the signature program at Christine's Hope, teaches citizens skills in baking and customer service. Their scrumptious cakes, cupcakes, cookies, brownies, nut rolls, and other treats can be ordered, purchased at local specialty food shops, catered at weddings, and sold by the citizens at pop-up stands during special events, like Cleveland Browns training camp.

Next, Bess tells me she is partnering on a retail storefront bakery right next door.

Did somebody ask about weekends? When the work is done, it's time to enjoy field trips together. How about a ferryboat ride to an island in the summer or picking apples at a farm in the fall? Just for fun!

We need more good-quality choices for young adults to build on the successes they achieved as students in school. Enduring support for people with lifelong special needs helps everybody find purpose.

Denise, Rita, and Bess have created the blueprints to make it happen.

Follow their lead.

Wash, wax, and shine on

Young Steve has good looks, personality, a big smile, and a disability you can't see. His typical outward appearance masks his intellectual disability, caused by a rare inherited condition known as Potocki-Shaffer syndrome.

When disabilities are easy to spot, it's easier to be kind. But people like Steve, with mild cognitive impairment, need kindness too.

He found his first full-time job after high school washing, waxing, and detailing cars. He loves cars. Knows everything about them. He even knows how to drive. Not bad for a young man who cannot read or write.

But when a new human resources manager joined the company, she challenged this disability she could not see or understand:

- How could he know which products to use if he can't read labels?
- How could he enter his time if he can't write?
- How could he pass online safety tests if he can't use a keyboard?
- How did he graduate from high school?

The answers are simple: Reasonable accommodations. Thank you, Americans with Disabilities Act. That's how he's able to do more than most might imagine.

He prepared for his driver's test by listening. A friend read the study guide aloud to him. During the exam, he listened through headphones to questions and multiple-choice answers. With a touch screen, he picked the right answer. On the road, he deciphers road signs as visuals. He listens to Siri for directions. Operating a vehicle? "I'm a natural," he says and smirks.

At work, products and labels are visuals too. He knows the blue window cleaner by its look and smell. Same for the pink soap. The wax? "Now that's obvious," he says with a grin. "Take a look and a whiff. That's wax! No doubt about it."

Entering his time is "a piece of cake," according to Steve, who can tell time and form numbers, a brain process quite different from decoding letters. That's why some of us are better with numbers and others with words.

Steve can learn, but not always in conventional ways. Accommodations, technology, and visuals help him learn, prove his knowledge, and become a productive and proud working citizen.

Steve left the culture of the car dealership for a better opportunity packing boxes at Amazon, where he can earn a livable wage, live on his own, drive a new pickup truck, and be married with no plans for children.

Oh, by the way, how did he graduate high school? With a mile-wide smile on his face as he walked across the stage and accepted his diploma, just like everybody else.

Our daughter has sprung a few strands of gray, clobbering me with an inescapable reality: Our perpetual child will grow old.

Who wants to live with the parentals forever?

Like many moms, I choked up when our first went off to college. Days later, he called home with a single question: "Does my yellow shirt go in the light or dark laundry pile?" I was ecstatic, confident he would be able to survive on his own.

But will someone please tell us how to let go of a child who never will? Our dark-haired daughter has sprung a few strands of gray, clobbering me with an inescapable reality: Our perpetual child will grow old.

It's tough for parents to envision the future for their children with special needs as they age. It's easier to predict what won't be. No spouse, no house. No kids, no car. And no worries.

As the saying goes, "It ain't all bad!"

When Noni was little, disappointments like these on the horizon crushed me, but not anymore. Time is kind in that way. Still, I wonder and worry. What's in store for my childlike daughter when, God willing, she turns 50 or 60? Simple math tells me her parents will be 80 and 90.

How old is too old to live with Mom and Dad?

Mapping out the rest of her life is the phase we're currently in. Today, she's content and safe at home with us, lounging in spa treatments as we pour bubbles into her bath, shampoo and condition her hair, shave her legs, trim her nails, clean her ears, and slather her in body lotion, all while her music plays. Sign me up! Did I mention regular pedicures at the salon for her signature brightly painted toenails dotted with white polka dots!

I'd feel better if living options for young adults with disabilities weren't so wanting. Have you been to a group home lately? They are not all equal, and I wouldn't park my goldfish in some.

Family friend Terry, with GLUT1 deficiency syndrome—a rare genetic condition causing intellectual disabilities, cerebral palsy, and seizures—was fortunate in his 40s and 50s to live happily in a top-notch group home. This lifestyle was the choice for many of his generation who never had an opportunity to attend school.

In his 60s, Terry needed more medical attention and moved to a robust senior living center with nursing care. He loves it there, and they love him. His eight siblings visit all the time and lovingly keep watch over him, honoring their parents' wishes.

For 20- and 30-somethings with disabilities, housing models are changing. Access to education, training, and community involvement has produced a more capable generation of young adults whose aspirations don't point to congregate living.

Many want to work at paying jobs in the community, attend church and sing in the choir, or go out for pizza after Friday night football games with friends and a little money in their pocket. Because they can. They can thrive with a greater degree of independence despite needing some level of care.

Society has been slow to anticipate this revolution. Here we are, more than thirty-five years of inclusion later, caught off guard with a scarcity of desirable housing options for this burgeoning population as they age. We need many more inspired spaces for adults with special needs to call home.

The rest of us take for granted the ample options we have when choosing where to live. In a house, apartment, condo, or tiny home? In the suburbs, the country, or downtown? In my dreams, on a boat on the water!

Kids with special needs become adults. Don't they deserve a nice place to live too?

We're stocking up on wrinkle creams to stay young until society catches up with the changing times.

Now it's the three of us

When your children are small, you can't go anywhere without them unless you get a babysitter. We've never gotten past this phase.

For forty years, we've not been free to leave our daughter without lining up someone to watch over her.

It was easier when siblings lived at home, but they've flown on.

The term "empty nester" often doesn't apply to parents of a child with disabilities. Most kids leave home sometime in their 20s, and it's a safe bet by their 30s they'll be outta there. Unless they can't fly alone. Unless they are totally dependent, like a nestling. That's my child. Perhaps that's your child too.

Not reaching empty-nester status has its ups and downs.

Our nestling is thriving happily at home. We enjoy her, and she enjoys us. We reap peace of mind doling out loving care for her in familiar surroundings.

She brings us joy. Every Halloween, she trick-or-treats house to house around the neighborhood, a few years as Tigger and last year as a cow.

Oh, what fun it is every December when Santa Claus comes to town! She still sits on his lap, watches for his sleigh in the sky, and thanks him on Christmas morning for presents under the tree. I'm wishing for Santa to drop the fountain of youth down the chimney so we can keep this lifestyle going for a long, long time.

In truth, day-to-day life is confining in ways most people never think about and most parents like us don't complain about. Wherever Noni goes, she is chauffeured. She's come to calling Daddy "my driver." Sometimes we joke that it's her turn to be our designated driver. "No, I can't," she reminds us. "I don't have my license yet. I'm still working on it!"

When friends call to invite us out, we say, "Sure, sounds like fun." Then we look at each other and think,

Who can watch Noni? Some friends welcome her to come along. Bless them.

Taking a long weekend or a short vacation just the two of us is a complex undertaking. Arrangements for her caregiving are elaborate and expensive, with pages of details for each day. Spur-of-the-moment is out of the question for us.

We recently scored some cheap airline tickets to Florida and took her with us, avoiding the hassle and cost of leaving her at home. She's become a good traveling companion, and we like exposing her to new places and experiences, but we won't have a single night out by ourselves. Hey, after she goes to bed, maybe we'll uncork a nice bottle of red wine. Delicious idea!

In the morning, we'll be back to our daily routine—making her breakfast, brushing her teeth, getting her dressed, fixing her hair, putting her shoes on the right feet—but instead of going to work, we'll be heading to the beach, feeling lucky.

Because this is our life.

Sit down, Mom and Dad

Our three adult children had something to say about their sister Noni's future when living with Mom and Dad is no longer an option. I mentioned a few potential housing options that might work, but they didn't like what they were hearing.

They sat us down, not to talk, but to listen. Here's what they had to say:

- "Would you like to know what *we* think?"

- "We don't like any of your ideas. No house sharing. No apartments. No group settings."

- "We want her to live in her own house, the house she grew up in, our house."

I assured them, "We're just looking ahead, gathering information. When it's time to make decisions, which won't be anytime soon, all of you will certainly be involved." That reassurance didn't sit well with them either.

"We've already made our decision," they countered, "but you aren't listening."

Noni has lived her whole life in the same house in the same neighborhood. The arrangement works fine for the three of us now. But for how long?

"For the rest of her life," according to her siblings, who shared their reasoning:

- "Someday, when you're not here to take care of her, she can still live at home with a caregiver and all of us living nearby."

- "We want to be able to stop over at the house for dinner, let our kids have a sleepover with Aunt Noni, bring beer, and watch Sunday afternoon football together."

- "You say she's not our responsibility. But she's our sister! We're always going to take care of her. Staying in the home and community she's familiar with is the best thing for her, and for us."

Hard to disagree with their point of view.

As parents, we've never wanted to burden our other kids with Noni's long-term care, and we've provided for her financially. But when the time comes, and we hope it's a long way off, nothing could be better for her than the idea they proposed. It's something we never would have asked of them, but couldn't be more grateful for.

We've just crossed the threshold into the decade of our 70s, still feeling young but wishing in this stage of life for a little more time away to take a trip, enjoy a weekend getaway, or do something spontaneous, just the two of us, without that nagging question: Who will take care of Noni?

"Would you kids be willing to help out now, so we could get away a little more often?" I probed.

"One hundred percent!" was their response. "One hundred percent, you two should enjoy some traveling. One hundred percent, we will help with Noni."

We took them up on the offer and ventured to Florida for a week by ourselves, leaving Noni in the good hands of her daytime caregiver, Marilyn, and our kids filling in at night and on the weekend.

We loved being away together, and we loved coming home to Noni in the family home.

It will always be hers, because we listened to her siblings.

Celebrating 40 in style

Noni's birthday is always festive, as it's the day before New Year's Eve. What better excuse for merrymaking!

When she turned 21, we introduced her to her first beer and were stunned when she chugged it before a cheering crowd. We should have known, because it's how she drinks everything poured into her glass. At breakfast, for example, she methodically eats all her eggs first, bacon next, followed by toast with jelly, then downs a whole glass of orange juice.

Over the years, we've marked her big birthdays with dinners, dancing, and dueling pianos in the company of adoring and imbibing friends and family. When the music plays, you can't miss her high-energy singing, grooving, and fist pumping. Before you know it, she wriggles her way on stage, exuberant, as the whole place sings "Happy Birthday" to her.

What's her favorite birthday present? Tickets to a musical.

She happens to share her birthday with LeBron James, and though she often forgets the date, she always remembers, "MyBron is my birthday buddy."

Turning 40, which seems unbelievable, launched her birthday shindig to new heights.

Hello, Nashville! Meet Noni! The new girl in town for the weekend.

The world's best siblings and their spouses planned a family travel adventure full of their sister's favorite things—live country music day and night, a wild party-bike outing, night bowling, and rounds and rounds of singing "Happy Birthday." While the rest of the world rang in the New Year, we raised our glasses to one special party girl who keeps us close.

Noni turning 40 signals Mom and Dad are getting older too. We're in a good phase of life enjoying our sweet girl. I can look back and know for certain the years of education, therapies, inclusion, accommodations, and advocacy, all mixed with love, got her and us to this place.

Hard work has paid off.

For parents approaching this phase, serious planning for an adult child's future without them is inescapable. We've done that planning, met with the lawyers and financial advisors, and lifted that heavy weight. With a sigh of relief, we feel good and more at ease.

Our plan for Noni is the "family home" option. She will continue to live in the small, familiar, and easily navigable ranch home she grew up in, with full-time caregiving and siblings nearby.

Our next worry? The doctor tells us it's time for her first mammogram and coming soon her first colonoscopy. Oh, crap! How we're going to get through these two procedures, I have no idea. But pretty soon, we'll get creative and figure it out as we always do. It's next on the list.

One thing I know for sure, it won't happen in the conventional way that works for the rest of us. We'll make accommodations. The story of our life.

Challenges that come along for Noni don't faze us anymore because, with forty years of experience, we're good at it now. Mammograms and colonoscopies? No sweat. We'll take it in stride and even joke about it.

If parenting is about celebrating the child you have, we're doing that.

"OPTIMISMS" TO LIVE BY

WE THINK of our kids with disabilities as our forever children, making it almost impossible to imagine them as adults. Growing up happens fast. The strategy and hard work that got you here is still the best way forward: Keep your expectations high and push for a bright, fulfilling adult life for your child.

Love Triumphs

The patience, resilience, and love I have learned to give has hands down made me a better human. This girl of mine, she is my world, my whole heart, and then some. But that doesn't mean this life isn't hard. It's okay to say that. Not for pity. Just my truth.
RACHEL ALVES, mother of Audrey, with CASK gene mutation

YOUNG COUPLE Rachel and Matthew Alves are on a parenthood journey they never imagined. Their only child—pretty, silly, sassy Miss Audrey Jo—at 10 years old is unable to talk and just learning to walk. "Our life is so different," observes Rachel:

- Sitting in silence, no spoken words
- Watching kids run at the park, not knowing what to say when they stare
- Filling the hours each day doing the same few activities she likes and can somewhat participate in

- Being exhausted every single day but getting up the next morning and doing it all over again
- Saying no to many gatherings she isn't able to tolerate and that simply can't work for the family
- Feeling guilty for not doing more, then feeling burnt out attempting to do it all

"We can have joy and frustration all wrapped together," Rachel explains. "We can love fiercely *and* wish things were different."

A trifecta of disabilities

Audrey Jo is not a baby anymore, and getting a 10-year-old in and out of her wheelchair many times a day is heavy lifting. For Rachel, working out has become a necessary part of her regimen to keep up with her growing girl.

Rachel is quick to describe her daughter as a giggly social butterfly with a delightful personality and great sense of humor. Audrey loves school, social settings, routine, books, animals, and being outside. She also uses a wheelchair, is nonverbal, and is incontinent, a trifecta of disabilities that can be overwhelming at times.

Parents of children with special needs experience more difficulty than most parents, but those whose children have multiple major disabilities have even more challenges.

Long after most youngsters learn to walk, Audrey is beginning to make slow progress. She can walk hand in hand for a short distance but fatigues easily, according to Rachel, who continues to see the need for a wheelchair with its heavy toll in the foreseeable future.

Audrey is learning to express herself in ways other than talking. "She is trapped in her body and her frustrations are high as she has so much going on in her little head," Rachel says. "We do everything imaginable to find other means for her to communicate."

Technology has produced some of the best solutions. Audrey uses an augmentative and alternative communication device programmed by Mom to enable her daughter to convey her needs and desires.

"She presses a button and I hear, 'Thirsty.' If I don't respond quick enough, I'll hear in rapid-fire fashion, 'Thirsty! Thirsty! Thirsty!' Okay," Rachel says and hops to it. "I guess you're really thirsty!"

Computer speak, however, delivers Audrey's words without intonation, which Mom misses. The words lack expressive meaning, such as surprise, anger, or delight. "What I would give to have her come home from school and tell me excitedly about her day," she wishes.

When Audrey outgrew her high chair and needed a larger specialized model, insurance denied the request again and again. Rachel stood fast. "Do you think I want this equipment for my child?" she quipped. "No parent does. I'd give anything for her to be able to sit and eat unaided on a chair at the table. But until that day comes, I have to fight for what she needs."

Relentless Rachel prevailed.

The next hurdle on the horizon? Potty training. Diaper changing becomes harder as children get bigger. "Often there's no place to change her, so we use the trunk of our car, taking care to preserve her dignity."

Who thinks about where to change the diaper of a growing child? Parents providing continence care for them do, along with some progressive organizations that believe it's about time we provide bathroom access for all.

Two campaigns, Changing Spaces in the United States, with chapters in most states, and Changing Places in the United Kingdom, are raising awareness of the need for more accessible changing stations. These campaigns push for powered height-adjustable universal changing stations in high-traffic public places like airports, shopping malls, theaters, museums, fair grounds, community centers, concert venues, stadiums, arenas, ball parks, and amusement parks.

In Ohio, the Cuyahoga County Board of Developmental Disabilities partnered with the Cleveland Metroparks Zoo to install an adult changing station accessible to all zoo patrons. In addition, a mobile van travels to outdoor events across the county, providing changing stations and calming sensory rooms for those who need them.

The organization is now working with the city's local businesses and professional sports teams to make them aware of this need and to provide grants and blueprints for getting it done.

Every day is physically strenuous and often exhausting for parents whose growing children are nonambulatory. Core-strength training is a must for them. They also rely on chiropractic adjustments, massages, heat packs, pain relievers, and safe-lifting practices.

Because they must be strong for their children.

Love letter to Daddy

On card-giving occasions like birthdays and holidays, I've always encouraged my children to write short and sweet messages inside. One might write, "Nanny, I like to go to your house for dinner." Or "Gramps, you have the biggest hands I've ever seen." Or "Poppy, I love to hear you yell 'Shoot it!' at my basketball games." Or, "Gramalee, I hope I grow taller than you."

Since Noni cannot write, she uses an ink stamp and exuberantly pounds "Noni" all over the card. It's her way of expressing her sweet thought.

But if she could articulate her feelings in writing, I imagine a letter to Daddy on Father's Day would go something like this:

Dear Daddy,

You loved me the moment you laid eyes on me. When you found out I wasn't as perfect as you first thought, you loved me even more.

You said it didn't matter. You said I'm yours, and if you have to take care of me forever, that's just what you will do. Furthermore, you said, you will love doing it.

You couldn't help falling in love with me. I made myself irresistible, wrapped snugly around your little finger. It's my most excellent splinter skill.

I practice it daily. When I have a choice to ride in Mommy's car or Daddy's truck, I always pick you. Then we turn up Led Zeppelin and the Allman Brothers while Mommy listens to her audiobook. Thank you, Daddy, for saving me!

When given the choice of staying home or tagging along with you, I always pick you. Because I love Home Depot! I'm fond of BJ's Wholesale Club too, where you buy your khakis for cheap. We laugh because we know Mommy hates them!

It's true, she's way better than you at making me look fashionable. She knows how to match clothes, work the curling iron, and supply me with scrunchies, blush, lotion, and lip gloss. But when she's not around, I like that we both can skip the fuss and just put on baseball caps. Hat day!

Vacations together are a blast, especially when Mommy goes shopping. I love it when you tell her, "The kid and I are going to the bar. Meet us there when you're finished. And take your time." Then comes a beer for you and water with lemon for me. Do I smell popcorn? How about another round? Twist my arm!

Under the breakfast table in the morning, I rest my foot on yours as I eat my oatmeal with blueberries and my English muffin with jelly. Then I make my way into your lap and kiss you on the cheek with my jelly lips. You know you love it!

We are living the good life, right, Daddy?

The sun rises, and you wake me up. The sun sets, and you tuck me in. You and me, me and you. Pure love.

Happy Father's Day to the luckiest dad ever.

Dear God

"Is something wrong with Noni?" elementary-school friend Libby once asked.

Her mom answered with a simple truth her young daughter could understand: Noni has an intellectual disability, making it hard for her to learn. Libby smiled with relief. "I'm so glad there's nothing wrong with her."

Libby and Noni became fast and forever friends in a third-grade inclusion classroom, when Libby wrote this letter to God, imperfect in its spelling, but perfect in every way that counts.

Dear God,

I have a new best friend! Her name is Noelle. She needs my help! I am going to do all of these things for her!

1. *pray for her*
2. *make sure she is safe*
3. *help her to rememper to sit [cross-legged]*
4. *ask her qestions*
5. *tell her what to do on a paper*
6. *help her learn letters*
7. *help her learn numbers*
8. *help her catch up in line*
9. *help her how to say f better instead of s*
10. *help her learn colors*
11. *help her how to pick up food and eat it*
12. *help her how to spell words*
13. *help her how to use her maners*
14. *help her how to write*
15. *help her how to read*
16. *tell her not to be afraid of big animals*
17. *help her how to run faster*
18. *help her how to count money*
19. *help her to look at numbers and say what they are*
20. *help her to learn like me*

I promise I will do this for Noelle!
Signed by an angel.

Autism meets its match

Greg and Noni met in an inclusive middle school that mixes students without disabilities with those with all kinds of disabilities, operating on the principle that inclusive schools lead to inclusive societies.

This environment brought together a reticent boy with autism and a social girl with developmental disabilities, like the magnetic pull of polar opposites.

Greg had no desire to participate in any school activities, despite everyone's coaxing. No parties. No dances. No sports. No clubs. No way. Autism kept him comfortable in his cocoon. Until he inched out, prompted by an unlikely source—Jason—Greg's rival for Noni's attention.

It was no secret that Jason was head over heels for Noni. His boisterous clapping and jumping at the sight of her gave him away. All the while Greg observed, rocking quietly and sometimes not so quietly.

But he couldn't stay an onlooker for long because of his heart's desire.

Greg ventured first to Saturday bowling and then to the homecoming dance, easing himself into the social activities that drew Noni, Jason, and their school friends together.

Stepping out senior year, he asked her to prom and post prom. The two social butterflies closed the place down at 4:30 in the morning!

When Greg's dad died suddenly, his family called us with a special request: Could Noni attend the visitation to be with Greg if he needed calming? They had made arrangements for a quiet room if he felt overwhelmed.

Clueless about autism, Noni sees nothing strange in Greg's behavior. She chats him up and he cracks her up.

The two sat together, with Noni's arm around Greg as he gently rocked. She looked at him and asked, "Are you sad, Greg?"

"Yes, Noni, yes, I am," he whispered. She put her head on his shoulder.

Years later as young adults, they are still close and look forward to bowling with a group of favorite friends once a week, high-fiving at strikes and spares, going nuts when one of them bowls a turkey, and altogether having a ball. Greg's soft spot for Noni trumps his social anxiety, motivating him from within, without anyone's pushing or prodding.

Clueless about autism, Noni sees nothing strange in Greg's behavior. She chats him up, and he cracks her up. When she senses he's feeling sad or agitated, she moves in nose to nose to calm him, obliviously invading his personal space. He lets her in, trustingly.

They are yin and yang, in disability and in friendship.

Everybody loves Brendan

Brendan makes quite a first impression.

For me, it was love at first sight. Same goes for a legion of friends and neighbors who adore this beautiful boy with Pfeiffer syndrome, a rare genetic disorder causing severe facial disfiguration.

Bren has a misshapen head, bulging eyes, hydrocephaly, intellectual disability, conductive hearing loss, and other anomalies. But, oh that smile! Mr. Personality makes friends wherever he goes, and he goes everywhere. His parents, Marti and Michael, have exposed him to a full life in our small suburban community.

He's a fixture at the rec center, lifting weights and flexing his muscles like Superman. He's ever present in his neighborhood on his flame-red three-wheel motorized scooter, dropping by to visit because when a neighbor says "Stop in anytime," he does.

Parties and dances? He's there. Community festivals? Count him in. Baseball, basketball, and football games? Oh, yeah. Cheerleaders? Better yet. He's never met one he wasn't head over heels for.

But it hasn't been an easy life for him or his parents. At 31, he's undergone more than forty surgeries literally from head to toe. That tally doesn't include many other hospitalizations for illnesses or complications.

"I stopped counting," says Marti. Her son lives with the aid of a shunt in his brain, a tracheostomy tube in his windpipe, and bone-conduction hearing aids worn on a headband. Fed through a G-tube in his belly, he's never tasted a morsel of food but is satisfied to sip a soft drink with friends.

He's already outlived his life expectancy.

How do parents cope with the stress of a medically fragile child destined for a short life? "We keep on loving him," answers Marti, "and we leave it in God's hands. It's all we can do."

Bren's daily medical needs limit his independence and his parents' freedom. For Mom and Dad to get away for a week, big sister Brittany moves in to care for her brother, and she's glad to do it.

Pfeiffer syndrome affects one in 100,000 people and, worn on the face, it can be a cruel disorder to live with. Sometimes, kids who encounter Bren for the first time are afraid of him. He loves little kids, so it doesn't take long for him to win them over.

Adults often stare. "I wish they knew better," Marti sighs.

Bren has made friends with others like him by attending annual summer retreats across the nation sponsored by the Children's Craniofacial Association. The association's national spokesperson, entertainer Cher, became involved after starring in the movie *Mask*, in which she played the mother of a child with a craniofacial condition.

Cher developed the idea of these retreats for families to interact, share ideas and experiences, and make lifelong friendships. In this atmosphere, everyone is accepted for who they are, not what they look like. Kids can run around and just be kids.

"You don't know what brave is," says Cher, "until you meet these kids."

Bren's bravado is always on display. Greet him with "Hey, Handsome," and watch him swagger, comfortable in his own skin and in the embrace of his hometown.

"He has faith," explains Marti. "He knows he's different. But he knows he's perfect in God's eyes.

"And he's perfect for me."

Here comes the bride—with a twist

"Always the bridesmaid, never the bride" is a familiar expression that aptly describes Noni.

One by one, her siblings have gotten married. She's been a bridesmaid in both her brothers' weddings and the maid of honor in her sister's.

Being maid of honor came with expanded responsibilities, like toasting the bride and groom, which required some assistance. Her brothers jumped at the chance to help Noni poke fun at Jacy on her wedding day. The boys regaled the bride with a litany of embarrassing stories, each one followed by the now infamous wisecrack from Noni, "G'luck, Johnny." With impeccable timing, she nailed it!

That all the siblings included her in their wedding parties melted my heart. So did the knowledge that my daughters-in-law and son-in-law wouldn't have it any other way.

When getting married is not an option, being a bridesmaid and maid of honor can suffice. We long ago accepted she'd never marry, but never anticipated her supporting roles would get her so close to the altar, joyously enough for her.

We thought it couldn't get any better until, for one shining moment, our maid of honor transformed into a bride right before our eyes. It happened at Jacy's wedding after the traditional father-daughter dance when Daddy was asked to remain on the dance floor.

What's happening? I wondered. I planned every detail of this event, and right now we were off script.

Suddenly, Noni appeared at the entrance of the ballroom adorned in an exquisite white gown of satin, tulle, and lace. Jacy took her hand and escorted her into Daddy's arms for a second father-daughter dance, this one to the Temptations song "My Girl." Little did we know, our scheming children and their spouses were all behind this sentimental surprise.

They gave their sister a moment to be a bride and share an unforgettable dance Daddy never thought he'd have with this special daughter. Watching the two sway was emotional overload of the best kind, sparking a standing ovation and happy tears all around.

We never imagined Noni would be a bride, but her siblings had other ideas that worked like magic. For Mom and Dad, a dream we let go of came true.

We witnessed another miracle for our girl.

When flags flew half-mast

Gregory was blue eyes and blond hair. Sunshine and smiles. Piano keys and knock-knock jokes. Peanut butter and jelly.

Gifted with great social skills, he was uber-involved in the community, and his aging parents did a good job keeping up with his calendar full of activities:

- Serving as an altar boy
- Attending public school
- Working like a pro at his job vacuuming at the JCPenney store
- Bowling for medals in Special Olympics, with a glove of his own
- Playing baseball and basketball
- Playing piano for hours, sometimes driving his mother nuts
- Dancing all night at homecoming, proms, and parties
- Eating lunch with varsity athletes, peanut butter and jelly every day
- Frequenting Friday-night football games sporting school colors

Gregory was smart. In school, he learned to read and write. His memory was sharp. Once he knew the date of your birthday or anniversary, he never forgot it. He'd always remind me whose birthday in my family was coming up next.

He liked to send friends handwritten notes and cards, always with a knock-knock joke inside. His too-cute face on a custom postage stamp adorned each envelope, so besides saving the notes, I saved the envelopes too.

Gregory lived, lived, lived life until he died of leukemia at 37. Individuals with Down syndrome, like Gregory, are more likely to develop leukemia than most.

Not even a dreadful disease could dampen his cheeriness. In the hospital receiving chemotherapy, he'd greet his nurses with "Hi, Beautiful! How's your day going?" When they, in turn, asked how he was doing, he'd grin and say, "I'm having a *great* day!"

It was impossible *not* to love this infectiously happy, lovable boy.

We dubbed Gregory "mayor" of our Special Olympics club because we always called on him to say a few words as our spokesperson or lead us in reciting the Special Olympics oath: Let me win. But if I cannot win, let me be brave in the attempt.

How appropriate when the *official* mayor of our town surprised Gregory at an annual fundraiser for special athletes, presenting him with a proclamation designating Gregory Mayor for a Day as the television cameras rolled. Unlike most recipients of proclamations, Gregory showed no restraint, jumping up and down with glee and waving his proclamation.

On his day in the mayor's office, Gregory's first act was to declare peanut butter and jelly the official food of our town, and so it is.

Sometime later, the mayor would accompany a group of Gregory's friends to visit him in hospice, where he ceremoniously gave Gregory the key to the city, under glass and beautifully engraved, treasured by his parents.

When Gregory died, city flags bowed to half-mast, a salute to a citizen mayor and a measure of a community's love for one special native son.

Looking back

One day, you'll have the joy of looking back on your life with your child and, like any parent, be able to reflect on the many ups and downs.

"What do you think when you look back on forty years of raising Noni?" I posed the question to my husband, seeking his perspective on the good and the not-so-good.

It took him a nanosecond to find the good:

- She's happy and living a great life, and we helped make it so.
- She inspired me to get involved in lots of sports and recreation activities for kids with special needs. I never would have become a community organizer if not for her.
- She's singlehandedly made our whole family better.
- Damn, I love that kid!

And the not-so-good?

- It's a lot of work—caring for her and creating opportunities in the community for kids like her.
- We don't have as much freedom or simplicity in our life as most people our age.
- We need a little break sometimes.

How would I answer the same question in a quick minute? Here's the good:

- She's given me clear purpose in life. I was meant for this.
- She's been a monumentally positive influence on her siblings, extended family, and friends.
- She's worked so hard, done surprisingly well, and made us proud.
- I'm happy she's ours.

What's not to like? Here goes:

- If I knew at the beginning how hard it would be to continually fight and advocate for her, I'd have thought, I can't do this! Yet I have.
- Her inability to do the simplest things for herself creates a ton of daily over-and-over work for us.
- She can stretch our patience.

We continually surprise ourselves with the lengths we will go to for our daughter. We take the good with the bad, grateful that forty years of loving her has made our family unimaginably stronger and closer.

Our tight bonds now extend to the next generation, our grandchildren, who embrace their aunt. When her namesake niece, Adelyn Noelle, 13, wrote an essay for school about her hero, we were touched to learn she had chosen Noni.

Forty years of loving her has made our family unimaginably stronger and closer.

My Aunt Noelle has CASK *disorder, so she can't read, write, drive, or tie her shoes. Even though she can't do some things, there are so many more things she can do. She learned how to ride a bike and competed in Special Olympics. She even has a job working at Heinen's.*

She has overcome so many challenges. Going to school was a lot harder for her than it is for most people, because she had to learn without being able to read and write, and that is not easy.

She always knows how to put a smile on anyone's face. For example, she calls my brother Lukie-Loo in front of all his friends to make everyone laugh.

If someone is not kind to her, she will still love you. Because of Noelle, I am a much kinder person. I always give people second chances and don't judge them, because you never know what's happening in their life.

When she doesn't get something on the first try, she keeps on trying. She has taught me to never give up.

She is my hero because she has changed so many lives.

Reading Addie's words describing Noni's role in her young life is just one of so many reasons we wouldn't change our experience for anything. Most parents like us feel the same way.

We don't get to choose the abilities or disabilities our children are born with. At some point, I stopped praying for a cure or a miracle to make Noni's condition go away. Now, I thank God for unanswered prayers.

Amen.

"OPTIMISMS" TO LIVE BY

WHEN YOU love someone with disabilities, you see perfection in a new way. Our children are perfectly imperfect, and it's loving them with all their imperfections that makes love unconditional and easy. Something you would have done anything to change turns out to be *someone* you wouldn't change for anything.

Acknowledgements

TO MY MOM, Lee Vrsansky, mother extraordinaire. I learned from you how to be a good mother.

To my husband, Rick. We are good together and have made something wonderful of this unplanned journey. I love that you are Noni's person. To Kale, Noni, Jacy, and Trent, my babes, my heart. I love how you love each other. To every member of our family: Noni's grandparents, aunts, uncles, cousins, nieces, and nephew. You embraced her from the start, and your ever-loving support means everything to us.

To Noni's teachers, aides, and classmates, from preschool through elementary, middle, and high school. You included our girl, and she thrived and achieved beyond our dreams. To our community: friends, neighbors, caregivers, coaches, mail carriers, Heinen's associates and customers, and the city of Middleburg Heights, Ohio, known as the friendliest city for those with special needs. You are our village, and we love you for it.

To my dear, departed friend Jackie Acho, whose book I quote in mine. You believed in me and propelled me to write this book. To AJ Harper, author of *Write a Must-Read*. Your advice set this first-time author on the right path.

To Emily Schultz, my editor at Page Two. We are a good team and my book is better for your ideas, precision, and sensitivity. To Jesse Finkelstein, co-leader of the pack at Page Two, my publisher. You saw the merit in my book from the start and stayed with me all the way.

To my Page Two team, my project manager, copy editor, publicist, and bookseller. I never knew how much went into publishing a book and appreciate each of your roles. To the designers, a talented bunch. Did I mention I love my book cover!

To members of the CASK Gene Parent Support Group on Facebook, devoted to helping each other. I hope my book raises awareness of our children's rare condition.

To families who shared stories of their children with me and families whose children are part of Noni's story. You have shown us how kids with all kinds of disabilities can lead bright, happy lives.

Shine On!

Notes

Preface

p. 3 *Disability is part of being human:* "Disability," World Health Organization, who.int/health-topics/disability.

p. 4 *one in six children aged 3 through 17:* "Developmental Disability Basics," Child Development, U.S. Centers for Disease Control and Prevention, May 16, 2024, cdc.gov/child-development/about/developmental-disability-basics.html.

1: It's Not the End of the World, but It Feels Like It

p. 5 Epigraph: Erma Bombeck, "The Special Mother," The Special Needs Child, the-special-needs-child.com/The-Special-Mother.html.

p. 11 *"getting the full brunt of parenthood":* Eliza Factor, *Strange Beauty: A Portrait of My Son* (Parallax Press, 2017).

p. 11 *"It's in moments of vulnerability":* Catherine Hong, "*Grey's Anatomy* Star on Raising Kids in Community," *Parents* magazine, updated December 19, 2022, parents.com/parenting/celebrity-parents/greys-anatomy-star-caterina-scorsone-on-raising-3-daughters-of-different-ages-and-abilities-i-would-never-perpetuate-the-myth-that-its-all-easy.

2: Let the Learning Begin

p. 21   Epigraph: Joan Raymond, "Temple Grandin on Her Struggles and 'Yak Yaks,'" *NBC News*, February 2, 2010, nbcnews.com/health/health-news/temple-grandin-her-struggles-yak-yaks-flna1C9442451.

p. 21   *"I had people in my life":* Raymond, "Temple Grandin on Her Struggles and 'Yak Yaks.'"

p. 29   *In the words of Temple Grandin:* Temple Grandin, "Interview with Dr. Temple Grandin," interview with Dr. Stephen Edelson, synapse, February 1, 1996, autism-help.org/story-temple-grandin-autism.htm.

p. 32   *"The biggest risk of not including":* Nicole Eredics, *Inclusion in Action: Practical Strategies to Modify Your Curriculum* (Brookes Publishing Co., 2018).

p. 33   *"Not every child in your class":* Eredics, *Inclusion in Action*.

3: Inclusion Lifts Us All Up

p. 37   Epigraph: "BookBrowse's Favorite Quotes," BookBrowse, accessed November 6, 2024, bookbrowse.com/quotes/detail/index.cfm/quote_number/433/use-what-talents-you-possess-the-woods-would-be-very-silent-if-no-birds-sang-there-except-those-that-sang-best.

p. 42   *"I have made friends with it":* Billie Eilish, "Billie Eilish Reveals She Has Tourette Syndrome," interview with David Letterman, May 2022 by Inside Edition, YouTube, 1 min., 46 sec., youtube.com/watch?v=h3e3XC4v-38.

p. 43   *"this century will mark a turning point":* Stephen Hawking, "Foreword," *World Report on Disability 2011* (World Health Organization, 2011), ncbi.nlm.nih.gov/books/NBK304077.

p. 48   *nearly twice as many boys:* "Diagnosed Developmental Disabilities in Children Aged 3–17 Years: United States, 2019–2021," U.S. Centers for Disease Control and Prevention, cdc.gov/nchs/products/databriefs/db473.htm.

4: Gifted and Talented? You Bet!

p. 53   Epigraph: "30 Best Eunice Kennedy Shriver Quotes with Image," BookKey, accessed November 6, 2024, bookey.app/quote-author/eunice-kennedy-shriver.

p. 53   *"You are the stars":* Eunice Kennedy Shriver, Charge to the Special Olympians at the opening ceremonies of the International Summer Games in South Bend, Indiana, August 1987, specialolympics.org/eunice-kennedy-shriver/media-library/remarks-1987-world-games.

p. 56   *the world of adaptive skiing:* Matt Masson, "Ride On! Winter Sports 2020 Guide," *National Geographic Traveller* (UK).

p. 64   *"Did you know picking up":* Jacqueline Acho, *Currency of Empathy: The Secret to Thriving in Business & Life* (The Acho Group 2021), 8.

p. 66   *novel communication method, Spelling to Communicate:* "Who We Are," International Association for Spelling as Communication, i-asc.org.

p. 67   *Speech-language pathologist Elizabeth Vosseller:* Elizabeth Vosseller, Growing Kids Therapy Center, growingkidstherapy.com/elizabeth-vosseller.

5: This Life Is Difficult

p. 71   Epigraph: Ernest Hemingway, *A Farewell to Arms* (Scribner, 1929).

p. 71   *"My brain is made up of":* Lisa Genova, *Love Anthony* (Gallery Books, 2012), 133.

p. 80   *They are three times more likely:* Cristina Novoa, "The Child Care Crisis Disproportionately Affects Children with Disabilities," Center for American Progress, January 29, 2020, americanprogress.org/article/child-care-crisis-disproportionately-affects-children-disabilities.

p. 80 *more expensive to send a child to daycare:* Baylee Patel, "The U.S. States Where Childcare Costs More Than College Tuition," *NetCredit*, August 31, 2023, netcredit.com/blog/cost-of-child-care-by-state.

p. 80 *at least one parent scaled back:* Erin Prater, "For Moms of Kids with Special Needs, Career Survival May Entail a Radical Pivot," *Fortune Well*, November 4, 2023, fortune.com/well/2023/11/04/special-needs-kids-mean-radical-career-change-working-moms-disability-parenthood.

p. 80 *American families reducing work hours:* Shaun Heasley, "Study: Families of Children with Special Needs See $18K in Lost Income Annually," *Disability Scoop*, October 28, 2021, disabilityscoop.com/2021/10/28/study-families-of-children-with-special-needs-see-18k-in-lost-income-annually/29569.

p. 85 *Her daughter... is prone to outbursts:* Emma Nadler, *The Unlikely Village of Eden* (Central Recovery Press, 2023), 207.

p. 85 *"both a spiritual calling and":* Nadler, *The Unlikely Village*, 207.

6: Think in New Ways

p. 91 Epigraph: Edie Weiner, "Thinking Technologies," The Future Hunters, thefuturehunter.com/our-work/thinking-technologies.

p. 91 *"We call this educated incapacity":* Weiner, "Thinking Technologies."

p. 93 *"All grown-ups were once":* Antoine de Saint-Exupéry, *The Little Prince* (Harcourt, Brace & World, Inc., 1943).

p. 97 *In the 1960s, upon learning:* "Camp Shriver—The Beginning of a Movement," Special Olympics, specialolympics.org/about/history/camp-shriver.

7: Say Hello to Giggles and Goofiness

p. 109   Epigraph: Dr. Konark Mukherjee, conversation with Cynthia Schulz.

p. 109   *"I meet parents of children"*: Dr. Konark Mukherjee, conversation with Cynthia Schulz.

8: Thank You to the Trailblazers

p. 123   Epigraph: Andrew Solomon, *Far from the Tree: Parents, Children and the Search for Identity* (Scribner, 2012), 46.

p. 123   *"In a 1927 Supreme Court decision"*: Solomon, *Far from the Tree*, 47.

p. 124   *"These parents have, by and large"*: Solomon, *Far from the Tree*, 47.

p. 127   *An ancient Chinese proverb:* "Tell me and I forget. Teach me and I remember. Involve me and I will learn. —Chinese Proverb," Illuminating Facts, illuminatingfacts.com/tell-me-and-i-forget-teach-me-and-i-remember-involve-me-and-i-will-learn-chinese-proverb.

9: Suddenly, They're Adults

p. 139   Epigraph: Sting, vocalist, "The Hiring Chain," 2021, by CoorDown, Small New York, Stabbilio Music, and Indiana Production.

p. 145   *"We provide a solution"*: "About Us," Aspire Accessories, aspireaccessories.com/pages/about-us.

p. 146   *"Just as we tailored school programs"*: "Our Stories," Blissful Seeds, accessed November 7, 2024, blissfulseeds.org/pages/about-us.

10: Love Triumphs

p. 161   Epigraph: Rachel Alves, interview with Cynthia Schulz, January 2024.

p. 171   *"You don't know what brave is"*: "Hidden Mask Interview —Cher," interview with Cher, Children's Craniofacial Association, 2011, ccakids.org/cher.html.

PHOTO: HOWARD TUCKER

About the Author

CYNTHIA SCHULZ is a voice to be reckoned with in the disability community. Forty years of experience as a mother raising a daughter with special needs has transformed her into a forceful advocate. After a longstanding career leading corporate communications, she has embarked on an encore career devoted to making life better for those touched by intellectual and developmental disabilities. Actively involved in her community, she currently serves on the Cuyahoga County Board of Developmental Disabilities in Ohio. She and her husband are parents of four adult children and five grandchildren, all living in Greater Cleveland. *Shine On* is her first book.

www.ingramcontent.com/pod-product-compliance
Lightning Source LLC
Chambersburg PA
CBHW060605080526
44585CB00013B/687